Stafford
Tales of

MYSTERY & MURDER

—— • David Bell • ——

COUNTRYSIDE BOOKS
NEWBURY BERKSHIRE

Cover designed by Peter Davies,
Nautilus Design

Produced through MRM Associates Ltd., Reading
Typeset by Mac Style Ltd, Scarborough, N. Yorkshire
Printed by Arrowsmith, Bristol

Contents

MAP OF STAFFORDSHIRE

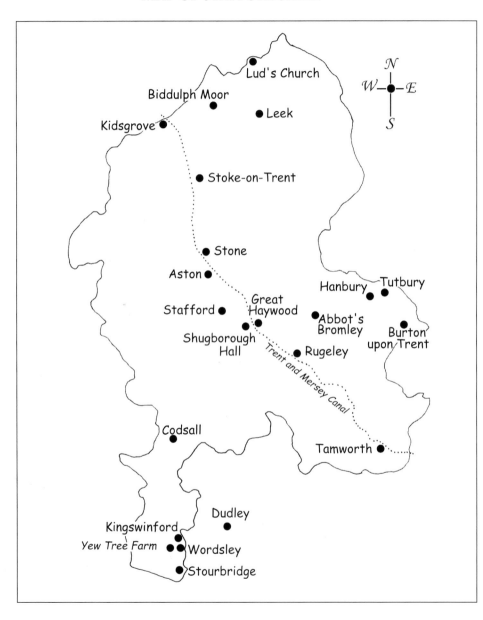

INTRODUCTION

———————❀———————

The twelve tales of mystery and murder contained in this book range throughout Staffordshire's history as well as its present. Among the mysteries are the phenomenon of the Leek double sunset which can be seen, weather permitting, every summer, and a look at the people of Biddulph Moor who believe they are descended from Saracen ancestors. There is a visit to the mysterious monument at Shugborough that may well have connections to the Knights Templar and the Holy Grail. Another visit is to a hidden ravine in the far north of the county regarded as the most magical spot in England, a location with both Christian and pagan legends attached to it. There is also a trip to Abbots Bromley where, every September, an ancient dance is performed in which 11th-century reindeer horns are carried.

One chapter deals with a hero from Tamworth, who lost his life in an action that may have shortened the Second World War by up to two years. His story, forgotten for six decades, has recently been recalled and at last he is getting the recognition he deserves. Another wartime event is recalled in the chapter that examines what really happened at Fauld, scene of the biggest non-atomic explosion of the war.

The murders include the case of a Codsall man assassinated by terrorists who were after his brother, a woman travelling by canal who was killed by drunken boatmen, and the Rugeley doctor who had a sideline in seduction, gambling and poisoning. Another case is that of a killer who decided to try kidnapping as part of his repertoire, and who revelled in the undeservedly glamorous nickname given to him by the press. There is also a detailed look at the murder of a schoolboy in south-west Staffordshire, which led to the wrongful conviction and imprisonment of four men.

David Bell

THE GREEN KNIGHT AND THE SECRET CHAMBER

❖

Lud's Church, sometimes written as Ludchurch, is not a building at all, but a ravine 200 feet long and 50 feet deep, hidden within Back Forest wood, close to the valley of the River Dane, between Swythamley and Gradbach. To the south lie the magnificent hills called the Roaches, and beyond them, the town of Leek. I went there on Midsummer Day 2004 with John Kay, a Swythamley resident with a deep interest in local history. We started out in heavy rain and returned in watery June sunshine. Walking through the wood, it would be quite possible to miss the entrance in the rocks, but when you do spot it, you climb down rough-hewn stone steps, curving down to the right. In the central chamber of the ravine it is about 10 feet in width, though it soon narrows again to about 6 feet. The climb out at the far end is a steep incline, and emerges onto open moorland.

This secret place is steeped in history and legend. Robin Hood, Friar Tuck and Bonny Prince Charlie are all reputed to have hidden from the authorities within the chasm, but its most famous connection is with a tale much older than the exploits of Robin Hood. This is the story of Sir Gawain and the Green Knight, first written by an unknown poet in the 14th century, and then incorporated by Sir Thomas Malory into *Le Morte D'Arthur*, his 15th-century prose collection of legends about King Arthur and his knights.

The original account was written in an old North Midland dialect, peculiar to Staffordshire, Cheshire, parts of West

Derbyshire and South Yorkshire, so it is likely that the author was from one of these counties. Dr David Clarke, in his Guide to Britain's Pagan Heritage, suggests that the poet may have been a monk at Dieulacres Abbey, near Leek. The other known works by this monk are strictly biblical, so why he should have written this very non-Christian tale od the Green Knight remains a puzzle.

The Gawain story probably originated at the time of Geoffrey Chaucer, but in a very different style, using alliteration rather than the rhyme used by the more southern poets writing for the court. The dialect and the older stylistic form suggest that Sir Gawain and the Green Knight was originally produced for a local North Midlands audience.

The saga begins with a wintertime feast held in King Arthur's court at Camelot, when a terrifying and mysterious visitor arrives. A wild looking giant rides his horse into the middle of the celebrations. Everything about the man – his flowing hair, his beard, and even his horse – is green. In one hand he carries a holly branch, in the other a huge battleaxe. In a deep booming voice, the giant challenges the assembled knights to play a violent game. One of them must strike him with his own axe, to cut off his head. In return the challenger will have to seek him out at his home – called the Green Chapel – and there submit to the same fate.

The knight who steps forward is Sir Gawain. He takes the heavy war-axe offered to him by the stranger and swings it with all his strength at the giant's neck. The severed head falls to the earth and rolls over and over on the flagstones, as the body collapses to the ground. Then the assembled knights gasp in amazement and horror as the headless man leaps to his feet, and picks up his head by its green hair. As he mounts his horse and rides out of the court, the eyes of the severed head flicker open, and the mouth speaks, reminding Sir Gawain to keep his side of the bargain in a year and a day.

The descent into Lud's Church. (Lesley Hextall)

The following November, Sir Gawain, a man of honour, keeps his promise, leaving King Arthur's side and riding north on his horse, Gringolet, to seek out the Green Chapel. His long and arduous winter journey leads him through

Wales into Cheshire. He has many battles on the way, fighting dragons, bears and wolves. By Christmas he is exhausted, hungry and cold. As he crosses the River Dane into the north Staffordshire moorlands, he finds in the middle of a wood a spectacular castle. Its owner, a red-bearded knight named Sir Bertilak, invites him in and treats him with great hospitality. Sir Gawain is able to eat and drink, and to rest until he regains enough strength to continue his quest. His host informs him that the Green Chapel he seeks is less than a mile away.

Bertilak tells Sir Gawain that he will be away hunting each day, but each evening he will return and exchange any animal he has caught for anything Gawain has won during the day. On the first day, while Bertilak is away, his beautiful young wife attempts to seduce Sir Gawain, and it takes all his knightly sense of honour and purity to resist her. She gives him one kiss, and when Sir Bertilak brings home a deer, Sir Gawain gives him the one kiss in exchange. On the second day Bertilak brings home a boar, and this time Gawain gives him the two kisses he has received from his host's wife. On the third day, the young woman attempts her seduction with even more ardour, and she kisses him three times. She persuades Gawain to accept a gift of her belt, which, she tells him, will protect him from all harm. When Bertilak returns with a fox, Sir Gawain decides to keep the magic belt, and gives his host only the three kisses.

On New Year's Day, Sir Gawain rides out to find the Green Chapel, wearing the belt under his armour. He rides through a wood, then finds the narrow entrance to a deep ravine. Gawain dismounts and walks down into the chasm, very conscious that he can hear the sound of an axe being sharpened. When he comes face to face with his old adversary, the Green Knight, he kneels and offers his neck. Three times the axe swings through the air. Twice it stops short, but on the third occasion it makes a small cut in the knight's neck.

Sir Gawain looks up to find the Green Knight roaring with laughter. He tells Gawain that he is actually Sir Bertilak and that, on his instructions, his beautiful young wife has been testing Gawain. He adds that the first two blows have stopped short because Gawain had told the truth on two days, when he really had nothing but kisses to exchange. The blow that inflicted the slight wound was to punish him for lying on the third day, when he had not handed over the belt. However, Bertilak now allows Gawain to keep the belt and he invites him to return with him to his castle, but the young knight feels ashamed of his deceit, and sets off on the long journey to Camelot, a chastened man.

The legend of the Green Knight of Arthurian legend was probably based on the ubiquitous Green Man who occurs throughout English medieval folklore as a fertility figure. Thus, Gawain's decapitation of this figure represents the annual 'death' and rebirth of trees, flowers and crops, the recurring cycle of nature. Some scholars have suggested that the story might represent the midwinter battle between the old sun god and the new one. Others see in the story a version of an old saga about the annual struggle between the Holly King (the Green Knight) and the Oak King (Sir Gawain).

The description of the Green Chapel in the story of Sir Gawain and the Green Knight so closely matches Lud's Church that scholars and literary researchers are convinced that the Green Chapel of the legend really was based on the north Staffordshire ravine. They believe that the original author must have known the chasm in Back Forest wood, and used the unique setting in his creation.

Another legend of Lud's Church dates from the early fifteenth century, when the Lollards – supporters of the doctrines of the early Protestant clergyman John Wycliffe – were challenging the established church. They were demanding an end to the extravagances of the clergy and a return to a bible-based religion. One of their main demands was for a bible printed in English that ordinary people could access, but this was regarded as outrageous. The King, Henry V, had declared the Lollards heretics and banned their services. Nevertheless, they continued to meet secretly, and one place that was ideal for the hidden meetings was the isolated ravine at Lud's Church.

The leader of the local Lollards was a 70-year-old man called Walter de Lud Auk. His name has led some to claim that Lud's Church was named after him, but according to local writer and newspaper editor Doug Pickford, it is more likely that Walter took his name from the place where he held his meetings.

On one tragic Sunday, Walter was preaching to his flock, safely hidden in the ravine. Guarding the narrow entrance was Henry Montair, the head forester, a devout Lollard and a man of huge stature. There were fourteen people taking part in the service, including Alice de Lud Auk, Walter's eighteen-year-old granddaughter. She was a beautiful girl with a pure singing voice, and her solos were much admired by the congregation, as Lollards always appreciated the human singing voice as a means of worship.

Despite the isolation of the spot, the king's soldiers had succeeded in tracking down this group of north Staffordshire heretics. They approached the entrance to Lud's Church and called out, commanding the worshippers to stop their service and surrender. Walter instructed his flock not to resist, but the giant Montair picked up the first of the soldiers and hurled him bodily back among his comrades. He called out to the Lollards to escape via the other end of the ravine while he held off their attackers. One of the soldiers fired a gun and the bullet whistled past Montair into the ravine. It struck Alice de Lud Auk, fatally wounding her.

As Walter and the other Lollards mourned the dying girl, the soldiers fell quiet. An hour later, they had the grace to allow Walter to bury the body of his dead granddaughter in the wood by the entrance to Lud's Church, and even stood by respectfully while the Lollards sang a hymn of mourning. Indeed it is recorded that some of the soldiers wept as the girl's body was lowered into the ground. After the simple funeral, the Lollards submitted to the soldiers, and were taken into custody. Most were imprisoned, but Montair managed to escape and fled abroad. It is believed that Walter de Lud Auk died in prison.

It is highly likely that Ludchurch was a place of worship long before the Lollards went there for their services, in fact well before Christianity came to the area. This amazing hidden place was probably used for pagan ceremonies in ancient times. Dr David Clarke, in his *Ghosts & Legends of the Peak District*, associates the Green Knight with the Celtic sun-god, Lug, and he thinks that Lud's Church may well be a corruption of Lug's Church. It is often claimed that the sun can only shine into the deep ravine on Midsummer Day, and this would certainly have led to pagan worshippers regarding it as a place of special importance. Although the cloud and rain prevented me from experiencing the sun entering the ravine on Midsummer Day in 2004, Doug Pickford and Andy Collins visited Lud's Church at midday on Midsummer Day 1993, and they were thrilled to find that the sun did indeed penetrate its depths. In his book *Earth Mysteries of the Three Shires*, Doug describes how the golden rays of the sun illuminated and warmed the chasm on that day of the summer solstice. The experience for Doug and Andy was both mystical and magical.

The path that leads to Ludchurch passes a strange rock formation, known as Hanging Rock. There are many legends associated with this spot too, including gruesome tales of human sacrifice. More mystical tales involve moon worship and contemporary visitors report seeing a hare that spends much of its time at both Hanging Rock and Ludchurch. The hare has long been associated in folklore with the moon.

Lud's Church is a mysterious and atmospheric place for any visitor, but for pagans it is even more special, more spiritual.

One young white witch, a follower of the Wicca path, tells me that, for her, Ludchurch retains all its ancient significance and power, present in the chasm for thousands of years. When I told her that I'd read of people taking away mud and clay from the Ludchurch area, in order to make good luck amulets, she disapproved. She firmly believed that the power should remain in its true place: at Ludchurch.

Another pagan, Willow, visited Ludchurch at Lammas (1st August) 2002 and found it awe-inspiring. She felt it was a place of death and rebirth, which certainly ties in with the Green Knight story. She also feels that it may have once been a place of initiation and sacrifice. She says, 'We saw faces and images in the rocks and crevices, and, being empathic, I had a feeling that a young man was once initiated there into the mysteries of the Goddess.' Willow tells me that Lud's Church 'came across as an entrance to the other world, and the womb of the mother earth.'

Another follower of the old ways is Sheena, who writes, 'I know that Lud's Church is what I call *one-of-those-places*, somewhere that seems to appear and disappear at will. What this means for me is that if I'm going looking for these places, they seem to vanish, and not want to be found. I put this down to the fact that I'm not meant to find them unless I'm ready. This has certainly been the case with both Lud's Church and the Bridestones. (Incidentally I've still not found the Bridestones, despite studying an Ordnance Survey map.)

'What I have discovered is that when these places do appear to me, and I do eventually find my way to them, they seem to reveal something strange. As in the case of Lud's Church. My arrival there, after many years of searching, proved fruitful one early summer's day in 2004. I eventually found Lud's Church, thanks to my current partner Gavin, who had spent a few months up there at a Scout Camp in the 1980s, helping with the refurbishment. We weaved our way across the bridge, and up the hill, feeling a sense of accomplishment that I would finally be able to view the enigma that is Lud's Church. We stopped off at Castle Rock, Gavin pointing out various places on the horizon, then we took the path into Lud's Church.

'I was amazed at the depth of the greenery there as I stepped down the slippery steps into the chasm. Gavin told me that it was around 100–200 yards long, and we made our way through. My only problem was that I couldn't progress beyond the halfway point. I became rooted to the spot, and couldn't bring myself to move forward. Instead we had to go back the way we came. I don't know what I encountered in there that day, but whatever it was it wouldn't let me walk through the cleft. I'm still puzzled by this, and obviously need to go back there and figure out what the problem was. I just got a huge sense of foreboding. I wasn't scared, but all the hairs on the back of my neck stood on end. I felt that it was a place of death, had some connection to the dead, maybe an Underworld passage. It was almost like a place to test oneself.'

KIDNAP AND MURDER

---❁---

In May 1972 the national press reported the case of a contested will. George Whittle, owner of a coach firm, had died and had left his money to his common-law wife Dorothy and their two children, Ronald and Lesley. His ex-wife was contesting the will, and the consequent publicity made the papers. Among the members of the public who read about the case was Donald Neilson. He was not interested in the rights and wrongs of the case, but he did mentally file the information that a young teenage girl, Lesley Whittle, had received a large sum from her father. Actually it was just over £80,000 but the media reports made it sound as though the family were millionaires. Three years later Neilson decided to kidnap the girl for ransom.

Donald Neilson had already killed three people and wounded two others during armed robberies when in 1975 he put into practice his plan to kidnap Lesley. Neilson was born Donald Nappey in 1936, but disliked his surname after being teased about it throughout his childhood and teenage years. He married at eighteen, and at nineteen he was called up for National Service. He became an infantry marksman and served in Cyprus, Aden and Kenya, before returning to civilian life. He bought a taxi from a man named Neilson and this was when he decided to change his embarrassing surname.

He was still obsessed with military matters and forced his wife and later his daughter to dress up and take part in war games on disused army bases. Replica guns were not enough for Neilson, so in 1971 he broke into a house and stole three shotguns and a hundred rounds of ammunition. In February 1974 he began a campaign of armed robbery, specialising in raiding sub-post offices. He was quite prepared to use violence. He shot dead sub-postmaster Donald Skepper in February, and seven months later he killed another postmaster, Derek Astin. The first two murders were committed in Yorkshire and Lancashire, but his third, only a month later, took place in Worcestershire, where he used a pistol to shoot dead a third sub-postmaster, Sidney Grayland. He pistol-whipped Mr Grayland's wife Peggy, then tied her up. Although Mrs Grayland was badly injured, she caught a glimpse of the killer when his mask slipped, and was able to describe a dark-haired man in his late thirties.

Because he always dressed in black, and was quite prepared to kill without compunction, the press decided to dub him the Black Panther. This was a pity. Not only was it an insult to a graceful and beautiful animal, it also gave some unwarranted glamour to a man who killed as part of his unglamorous chosen career as a thief. I will not be using that sobriquet in this book.

Robbery was not proving to be as financially rewarding as Neilson had hoped, so in January 1975 his mind returned to the Whittle family. He decided to kidnap Lesley Whittle, now aged seventeen, and demand a ransom of £50,000 from her family. He knew of a place in north Staffordshire where he could hide her: a drainage shaft beneath a park in Kidsgrove.

When Dorothy Whittle went into Lesley's room on the morning of Tuesday 15th January, her daughter was not there. Her disquiet increased when she realised that the only clothes missing were a nightdress, a dressing gown and slippers. This meant that Lesley had disappeared without any outdoor or normal daytime clothing. Dorothy searched the whole house in vain, then tried to ring her son who lived nearby, but she found that her telephone was not working. In fact, the kidnapper had cut the wires at 4 am when he had taken the terrified girl. Dorothy went to tell her son of his sister's disappearance, and brought him back to her house.

In an empty chocolate box, which had been placed on top of a vase, they found a message from the kidnapper. This was neither handwritten nor typed; it was impressed onto Dymo tape. The chilling words read: NO POLICE £50000 RANSOM BE READY TO DELIVER FIRST EVENING WAIT FOR TELEPHONE CALL AT SWAN SHOPPING CENTRE TELEPHONE BOX 64711 64611 6311 6PM TO 1AM IF NO CALL RETURN FOLLOWING EVENING WHEN YOU ANSWER CALL GIVE YOUR NAME ONLY AND LISTEN YOU MUST FOLLOW INSTRUCTIONS WITHOUT ARGUMENT FROM THE TIME YOU ANSWER THE TELEPHONE YOU ARE ON A TIME LIMIT IF POLICE OR TRICKS DEATH

A second Dymo tape told them how the £50,000 was to be made up of used notes, half the amount in £1 notes, the rest in £5 notes. It also said that the victim would only be released after the money had been paid.

Despite the warning opening words of the message, the West Mercia police were called. The detective in charge was Chief Superintendent Bob Booth, a man with a tremendous record of solving crimes, a detective who had successfully got to the bottom of every one of the seventy murder cases he had investigated.

Bob Booth quickly established that Lesley's disappearance was not a stunt, nor had she run away with a boyfriend. It was a genuine kidnapping. He thought at first that she might be being held locally in a caravan or a nearby house, and a search with helicopters and dogs began. However, the notion that she was still a prisoner in the immediate neighbourhood was wrong. Lesley had already been taken to the drainage shaft under Bathpool Park in Kidsgrove, where she was standing on a narrow ledge and tethered by a wire noose around her neck. Bob Booth already knew that the man who had kidnapped the girl was a callous criminal, but even he could not have guessed just how vicious and uncaring the man could be.

The plan was to keep the police involvement a secret. Bob Booth arranged for the £50,000 ransom money to be withdrawn from the bank, and for Ronald Whittle to take it to the Swan Shopping Centre as the kidnapper had instructed. The banknotes had been photocopied for future identification purposes, and undercover officers were placed to watch Ronald as he waited for one of the phones to ring. However, things went badly wrong. News of the kidnapping was broadcast on the television news at 9 pm, and a police officer aborted the procedure. When the kidnapper rang at midnight, there was no one to receive the call. Bob Booth was horrified and furious. The operation had been abandoned without reference to him, and he knew very well that the television news broadcast might mean the death of the kidnapped girl.

Bob Booth decided to send Ronald to the same phone box on the following evening, in hope that the kidnapper would ring again, but the officer was outraged to find the kiosk surrounded by reporters and photographers. The press compounded their folly by making the outrageous suggestion that Ronald Whittle might have been the kidnapper of his own sister.

On the same evening as the second unsuccessful visit to the phone box at the Swan Centre, an apparently unconnected crime took place 30 miles away in Dudley. Gerald Smith, a security guard with British Rail, approached a man who was lurking near the freightliner depot. The man shot him down, then walked over to the wounded guard and tried to shoot him again at point blank range. Fortunately the gun failed to fire this time and the man ran off. Examination of the bullet fired at Gerald Smith proved to be the same type as those used to kill the sub-postmasters murdered earlier.

In the meantime, the kidnapper had been in contact again. Len Rudd, the transport manager at the Whittle coach company answered a call, which he knew from the pips was from a call box. To his amazement and joy he heard the voice of Lesley Whittle. As he tried to speak to her, her voice continued and he realised he was listening to a tape recording. Her voice said, 'Mum, you are to go to Kidsgrove post office phone box. The instructions are going to be inside. I'm okay but there are to be no police and no tricks, okay.'

The police wired up Ronald Whittle with a microphone and he set off for north Staffordshire. At Kidsgrove he found the post office and began to search the phone box. Eventually he located a message hidden behind the backboard, which told him to go to a particular point in Bathpool Park at midnight and look for a flashing light. He would find a torch with further instructions fastened onto it. Ronald immediately drove to the park but to his despair he was unable to find any flashing light. Once again the trail had turned cold. Bob Booth sanctioned Scotland Yard officers to make a discreet search of Bathpool Park but they reported that they had found nothing.

A week after the Dudley shooting, the police found an abandoned stolen car with false number plates, only a few hundred yards away from where the incident had occurred. Evidence in the car – including more Dymo tapes and a second cassette tape with Lesley Whittle's voice – proved that it was not only connected with the shootings but also with the Lesley Whittle kidnapping. For the first time, the police now knew that the kidnapper was a man who had already killed three times. It fell to Bob Booth to break this news to the Whittle family.

Booth wanted to take a closer look at Bathpool Park himself, but was deterred by the fact that if the police went there openly and in numbers, the kidnapper would realise that the police had been involved from the beginning. He therefore arranged for Ronald Whittle to give a television interview on *Midweek*, where he would suddenly reveal how he had gone to Bathpool Park but had failed to make contact with the kidnapper. Bob Booth, who was being interviewed in the same programme, feigned outrage at this 'revelation' and terminated the interview. The police now had a legitimate reason to search the park.

On 7th March children playing in Bathpool Park found pieces of Dymo tape and a torch by the entrance to a drainage shaft that they knew as 'the Glory Hole'. There were actually three of these drainage shafts and Bob Booth ordered that they should be searched. Two proved empty, but at the third, on a metal grill 50 feet down they saw a mattress, a blanket and a sleeping bag. Detective Constable Philip Maskery went down to the narrow shelf, and by the light of his torch, he caught sight of a blue dressing gown. He shone his torch further down the shaft and saw the naked body of Lesley Whittle, hanging from a metal cord round her neck.

As the death had occurred in Kidsgrove, the Staffordshire police now took over the investigation. Bob Booth fought to continue with his team but they were sidelined, and he was no longer in charge of the case. Bob's disquiet was increased when he learned that a witness came forward with evidence that a Staffordshire police panda car was in Bathpool Park at the time when Ronald Whittle was trying to make contact with the kidnapper.

Donald Neilson.

Peter Shorto, a local DJ, and his girlfriend were parked in the park at 2.45 am but their courting was interrupted. First a torch was flashed on and off a few yards in front of their car, which Peter thought might have been someone walking a dog. Then headlights swept across the park, and a car pulled up nearby. The driver lit a cigarette, and Peter commented to his girlfriend that it was just a policeman stopping for a smoke. Fifteen minutes later, a van drove into the park, parked in front of Peter's car, flashed its headlights, then left, driving off at speed.

Bob Booth concluded that the presence of a police car in Bathpool Park that night had panicked the kidnapper, and that this had caused him to return to the drainage shaft that night to push the tethered girl off the ledge. Although Staffordshire police denied that any of their cars were in the park that night, Chief Superintendent Booth remained sceptical.

It was mid-December before Donald Neilson was captured, and then his arrest occurred only because he had gone back to robbing post offices. Two Nottinghamshire police officers were parked when one of them, PC Tony White, spotted a man acting suspiciously near a post office. His colleague, PC Stuart McKenzie, drove up to the man and Tony White began to question him. The man began by saying his name was John Moxon, but suddenly produced a shotgun and aimed it at PC McKenzie's head. He ordered PC White to get into the back of the car, then climbed in next to the driver, pointing the gun at his chest.

After driving for some time, Stuart McKenzie decided that the man would probably shoot them both dead. He had to take some action. As they neared the village of Rainworth, he suddenly swerved right, then left, braking at the same time. The gun went off, and Stuart threw himself from the car. He heard Tony shouting that he had been shot in the hand, and hurried round the car to help. He saw that Tony was holding the gunman round the neck and was thumping him with his elbow. As the two officers struggled with Moxon, they were joined by local man, Roy Morris, who raced from a local chip shop to help them. They managed to handcuff the gunman and chained him to some railings. More locals came out to help, and in the end the two police officers had to protect their captive from being hit by the civilians.

In Moxon's holdall, the police found torches, knives, razor blades, a bottle of ammonia and a black hood. Moxon refused to speak to the police for two days, but then confessed that his name was not John Moxon but Donald Neilson. In the attic of his Bradford home, the police discovered maps and car keys, more black hoods, a sawn-off shotgun, and a Dymo machine. One of the letters on the machine was off centre, and it was easy to prove it was the machine that had punched out the messages used in the kidnapping of Lesley Whittle. The police were sickened and disgusted when they also found a model black panther. Donald Neilson had obviously revelled in the press attention and had really loved it when they called him the Black Panther.

At his trial in July 1976, Neilson was charged with thirteen violent crimes, four of them murders. He admitted that he had robbed the post offices where the men had been shot. He also admitted that he had kidnapped Lesley Whittle and held her in the drainage shaft in Kidsgrove. Neilson seemed to enjoy his time in court, and willingly donned his black balaclava mask, showed how he had held his shotgun, and even demonstrated how he had put the wire round Lesley's neck. He claimed that he had not killed Lesley deliberately, but had accidentally pushed her off the ledge. Whether any of the jury might have believed this version of the events is doubtful, but he then stretched credulity even further by claiming that his gun went off accidentally in each of the robberies where a man died. He was not believed and the jury took only 90 minutes to find him guilty of the kidnap and murder of Lesley Whittle, and of the murders of sub-postmasters Donald Skepper, Derek Astin and Sidney

Grayland. He received five life sentences, and has been told by the Home Secretary that he will never be released.

During the trial, Bob Booth upset his police colleagues by telling the court his belief that there genuinely was a police car in Bathpool Park on the night when Ronald Whittle was trying to contact the kidnapper, and that this had led to Lesley's murder. He also revealed for the first time that Scotland Yard had been involved in the ransom run, and that they had made the incompetent first search of Bathpool Park. Detective Chief Superintendent Bob Booth paid a price for his outspoken views. Because of what was seen as disloyalty to the police force, he was dismissed from the CID and returned to uniform. However, it is not the damage to his career that still haunts him, but his failure to find Lesley alive. In an ITV documentary programme in 2002, Bob Booth stated, 'We let that girl and the Whittle family down.'

THE LEEK DOUBLE SUNSET

———— ❁ ————

First recorded in the 17th century, the Leek double sunset attracts visitors every summer solstice, because, for a few days in June, the sun first sets behind a local hill called the Cloud, only to reappear lower down on the other side of the hill. It then sets for a second time on the horizon. This phenomenon has always fascinated people, and visitors gather in the Leek area to try to view it every year. The traditional spot for viewing (though its relevance today is considered later) is the churchyard of St Edward the Confessor, and in particular the part in the north-eastern corner known as Doctor's Corner, where the graves of eight surgeons are situated. The time for visiting is usually Midsummer Day, although the days just before or just after are also possible.

The phenomenon has been known for some time. In 1686 Dr Robert Plot wrote: '*To come then to the subject in hand, the Natural History of the County of Stafford; the first thing I met with relating to the Heavens, and one of the first too that I heard of after I set to work in earnest, was a pretty rural observation, of late years made by some of the inhabitants of the town of Leek in the moorlands, of the setting of the Sun in the Summer solstice, near a hill called the Cloud, about six miles distant, in the confines of Staffordshire and Cheshire; which appearing almost perpendicular on the northern side, to such persons as are standing in Leek churchyard, the sun seems so nicely at that time of year to cut the edge of it at setting that notwithstanding what is taught by Astronomers, that the sun whilst it occupies that cardinal point, appears stationary for some time without giving any sensible increase or decrease to the length of the days; they can plainly perceive by the help of this hill, that no two days are equal, but that there is a sensible difference every day.*

'*For when the sun comes near the solstice, the whole disk of it at first sets behind the hill, after a while the northern limb first appears, and so every night gradually more, till at length the whole diameter comes to set northward of it, for about three nights; but the middle night of the three, very sensibly more remote, than the former of the following, when beginning its recess from the Tropic, it still continues more and more to be hidden every night, till at length it descends quite behind it again.*'

Although Dr Plot was an academic and a scientist – he was the professor of chemistry ('*chymistry*') at Oxford University and the first keeper of the Ashmolean Museum – it is possible that he was describing the Leek double sunset from hearsay and that he had never actually seen it. Certainly in the illustration in his book, showing the sun reappearing from behind the Cloud, the hill bears little resemblance to its real shape. Jeff Kent, a Staffordshire author leading researcher into the double sunset, believes that Robert Plot never witnessed the phenomenon himself but was writing using secondary sources.

The shape and position of the Cloud, also known as Bosley Cloud, is vital in causing the double sunset. Viewed from the east – from the Leek side – the southern side of the Cloud is a very gentle slope but the northern side falls away steeply. In midsummer, the sun can be seen to set just to the south of the hill's summit. It remains hidden for a while, only to reappear from the northern steep side. It then continues to set once again on the horizon at the foot of the hill.

Another illustrated article appeared in *The Gentleman's Magazine* in 1738. This states that the Cloud '*is so situated with respect to the churchyard of Leek that a spectator standing there of an evening three or four days before the*

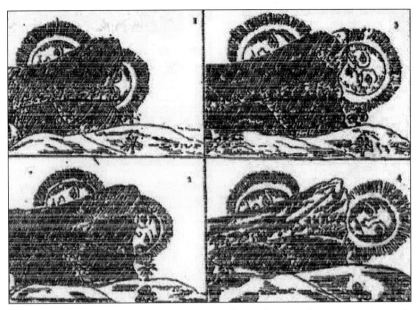

A woodcut showing the double sunset from the Gentleman's Magazine, 1738.

10th of June, beholds the disk of the sun gradually emerging from beyond the northward side of the hill.' The date of 10th June given for the double sunset seems odd, but it must be remembered that the Gregorian calendar, which removed eleven days, was adopted fourteen years after this article was published. This makes the date that of our modern Midsummer Day, 20th/21st June. Once more the illustration to the article does not show the genuine shape of the Cloud, again suggesting that the illustrator had never visited Leek!

Every year at the summer solstice, people gather at the church in Leek in hopes of watching the sun set on the Cloud, then a second time at the horizon. They are now invariably disappointed. Obviously the weather plays a part, if it is raining or cloudy the sunset is not going to be seen. Another problem is caused by the trees planted in the 1960s by the church authorities. These have now grown dense enough to prevent the viewers from getting a decent sightline of the Cloud, and may have been deliberately placed to do so. Certain churchgoers regard the watchers as non-Christian, and therefore resent their pagan presence in the churchyard. Jeff Kent does not agree with this reading of what happened, and tells me that he finds members of the church very helpful. He points out that some of the obscuring trees lie outside the churchyard, and are owned by the council.

Yet a third problem is arising, caused by the fact that the angle needed to observe the double sunset has altered over the centuries. This is said to be due to the 'changing obliquity of the ecliptic', which I believe refers to apparent changes caused by the innate wobble in the axis of the earth.

Kevin Kilburn is an astronomer with an interest in archaeoastronomy, which means that he uses his academic researches to discover how the stars and planets would have appeared to people in the past. In articles published in the journal of the Royal Astronomical Society and broadcast on BBC Radio 4, he has examined the Leek double sunset. He concludes that 2,000 years ago the double sunset would have been visible from what is now the south-west corner of the churchyard, whereas 1,000 years ago it could be viewed from the newly built church itself. In Dr Plot's time, the optimum point viewing had moved north-eastwards, and in recent years it has been seen only from the farthest north-east corner of the churchyard. He also forecasts that within 25 years the double sunset will not be visible from its traditional churchyard observation ground, and this disappearance will last for well over twenty thousand years! This means that, even if the problem of the churchyard trees can be overcome, the time is approaching when the famous double sunset cannot be seen from this location. The church and/or civil authorities might perhaps be persuaded to cut back their trees, but of course nothing can be done about the variations caused by the changes to the angle of tilt of the earth's axis.

That is bad news for the hundreds of people who wish to observe the Leek phenomenon, but there is good news too. The double sunset can be seen from other parts of the town. Jeff Kent and twelve companions were delighted to see the 2004 double sunset from a point on the road to Pickwood. Their pleasure was made even more intense because no one had seen the double sunset from Leek on the summer solstice since 1977. 'The conditions were perfect,' he said. 'We saw the whole of the sunset at 9.32 pm, on the summit of the Cloud, some seven miles away to the north-west. Ten seconds later, the first chink of light appeared off the northern scarp slope of the hill. The sun increasingly reappeared until approximately 20% of it came into view. It rolled down the scarp before setting for the second time at the base of the hill at 9.36 pm.' Before going to his viewing point, Jeff usually calls at the churchyard, but is unable to persuade all the crowd gathered there to come to where he knows they would stand a real chance of seeing the double sunset. 'Some people don't seem too impressed with the sight of a long-haired stranger telling them they are in the wrong place,' he told me. 'Tradition dies hard.'

Other viewing points that Jeff recommends are listed in his book *The Mysterious Double Sunset* and include Lowe Hill and Pickwood Vale Recreation Ground. Outside Leek, Jeff recommends a spot at Woodhouse Green on the summer solstice. This position has the advantage of being much closer to the Cloud, so that the hill appears larger in comparison to the sun than when seen from Leek. If the observer does not mind seeing the hill on dates that do not coincide with the midsummer solstice, then the choice of viewing locations is even wider. On 17th July 2004 I went with Jeff and about twenty others to attempt to witness a potential quintuple sunset (!) from a point west of Rushton Spencer, but although we held our breath as the sun approached the Cloud (with a capital C), we were defeated by clouds (with a lower case c).

However, even if we had been successful, the purists would not have been impressed, as it was not the summer solstice and we were not in the Leek churchyard. For some, it has to be just one particular spot and just one specific time of year. The church of Edward the Confessor was built in the early 14th century, but there is strong evidence that there was an previous church on the same location, which burned down in 1297. What was there before that church is a subject of debate and disagreement. Kevin Kilburn believes that there may well have been a pagan place of worship on the spot for thousands of years, and it is true that many early Christian churches were built on sites sacred to the older religion. The church is situated on one of the highest parts of Leek and, given the view of the midsummer double sunset, it would have certainly been regarded as a very special place. Many others agree, including Doug Pickford, local author and newspaper editor, and the late Harold Bode, who was a local historian and once a fellow-headteacher of mine in a north Staffordshire village school.

However, Jeff Kent suggests that the rare occurrence was first noticed by Viking invaders in the late 9th century and points out the lack of any evidence of a prehistoric pagan site. He strongly believes that pre-Christian people were in touch with natural events and would not have regarded the double sunset with superstitious awe. Jeff also stresses that people are incorrect to say that the Leek church viewpoint of the double sunset is unique. The Cloud double sunset is visible from other places and, moreover, there are other hills that produce the same phenomenon. On the other hand it might be argued that the double sunset on the Cloud as seen from St Edward's in Leek is the only case where the phenomenon can be viewed from a sacred site. The argument continues!

DEATH ON THE CANAL

———————❧———————

Christina Collins met her death in Rugeley as she travelled along the Trent and Mersey Canal in 1839. Christina had been born in Nottingham, the daughter of an inventor of machines for lace-making and the manufacture of fishing nets. The trade of inventor was a precarious one, and although the family was occasionally prosperous, they were on parish relief by the time of her father's death in 1818. Christina's mother was forced to find work as a nurse, and worked as such until she was past sixty.

Young Christina married Thomas Ingleby, a man many years older than her. Perhaps she was dazzled by his lifestyle, because Thomas was in showbiz! He was in fact a well-known stage magician known as 'The Emperor of all the Conjurers'. He lived a nomadic life, touring the country and performing at theatres throughout the land. His stage show was not for the squeamish. One of his feats was to slaughter a chicken on stage by cutting off its head, pass the bloody head round the audience to prove its authenticity, then miraculously resurrect the bird (actually a second chicken) and send it strutting around the stage. He would perform a less callous version of this trick in which he borrowed a pocket watch from a member of the audience, pounded it into pieces, then restored it to its original condition before returning it to its owner. He also included an act involving the devouring of knives and forks.

Christina joined her husband on his travels and became part of the act, adding singing and dancing to the performance, and later participated in the conjuring tricks.

The couple had no children. When Thomas Ingleby died in 1832, he left Christina an attractive young widow aged 30. Some years later Christina fell in love with and married Robert Collins, a man of her own age this time. The couple moved to Liverpool to find work, but although Christina found a position as a seamstress in the house of a Mrs Grice, Robert was less successful. In 1839, Robert left Christina in Liverpool while he went to London to seek work. His luck seemed to improve, because within a week he had found work as an ostler and taken lodgings in Edgware Road. Immediately he sent a guinea to his wife and asked her to join him in London. Christina was delighted and took leave of her employer. She put on her blue silk bonnet, and set out on the long journey.

She did not have enough money to travel by stage coach, or by the newly opened railway, so she took the cheaper but much slower alternative. She made her way to the northern end of the Trent and Mersey Canal at Preston Brook, and paid the sixteen shillings fare to travel to London on a boat belonging to Pickford and Co. The captain of the boat on which Christina embarked was James Owen, and the crew consisted of two men, George Thomas and William Ellis, and a boy, William Musson.

At 7.30 pm on Saturday 15th June, the boat set off on its journey south. The route to London should have led through Stoke-on-Trent and Rugeley to Fradley junction, where the boat would take the Coventry Canal and continue via Oxford. However, the vessel had not travelled far before Christina began to have trouble from the rough, and often drunken, crew. They obviously found the petite and handsome young woman a subject of lecherous fantasy, and took malicious pleasure in telling her so. By the time the boat had reached Stoke-on-Trent at midday on Sunday, Christina was so frightened that she complained to William Brookes, a Pickford's porter, about the behaviour of the men.

She also enquired about the possibility of continuing her journey from Stoke to London by stage coach, but found that no suitable coaches were available. Reluctantly she rejoined the boat and its unpleasant crew. To reassure her, William Brookes' wife travelled on the boat with Christina Collins for the next few miles, and the crew kept their conduct under relative control, but once Mrs Brookes got off, Christina was alone with the men again. At Stone, she complained to a Trent and Mersey check clerk that the crew were so drunk that she was frightened they intended to 'meddle with her'. The clerk was not very concerned and he advised the frightened passenger to report the men's misconduct when she reached her destination. That advice turned out to be particularly callous and unhelpful.

The canal boat did not travel very fast, and Christina decided to walk along the towpath for a while, intending to get back on board when the men were more sober. At the lock-keeper's cottage at Aston, she was seen sharpening a penknife on some stone steps, presumably intending to use it for self-protection. When the boat arrived, one of the crew was heard shouting abuse at her. However she had no choice but to re-embark, and was seen to refuse a drink proffered by James Owen, the captain.

At about 9 pm, another Pickford's boat passed, and its captain exchanged words with James Owen. In vulgar language, Owen described what he would like to be doing with his female passenger that night. The terrified woman was seen taking another solitary walk along the towpath at 10 pm by another boat captain. At midnight, the lock-keeper at Hoo Mill was awakened by a woman screaming. He and his wife looked through their window and saw three men by a boat. A woman was sitting on top of the cabin, crying, 'I will not go down!' The lock-keeper's wife asked the men who the woman was, and the captain replied that she was a passenger. He also claimed that the woman's husband was travelling with her. This was, of course, a blatant lie.

That was the last sighting of Christina Collins alive. A boatman, Thomas Grant, found her dead body in the canal at Brindley Bank near Rugeley at 5 am the next morning. She was floating face down in the water, on the opposite side of the canal from the towpath. Grant stopped his canal boat and used a hook to tow the body over to the path. Her face was completely black. With the help of a passer-by, John Johnson, Grant got the body out of the water and took it to the Talbot Inn in Rugeley. The dead woman, who was wearing no shoes and no bonnet, was still warm when taken from the canal.

When the Pickford agent heard of these events, he sent for the police, and the four crewmen were arrested by a constable when the boat reached Fazeley. Following a coroner's inquest held at the Talbot Inn, the boatmen were charged with the rape and murder of Christina Collins, and sent to the county gaol in Stafford to await trial. The boy, William Musson, was originally accused along with the three adult members of the crew but he was released without charge before the trial.

The first trial was held in July before Mr Justice Williams. The prosecution outlined the rape charge first, but the judge ruled that there was no evidence that the men had raped the victim and ordered the jury to bring in a verdict of not guilty. The prosecution asked the judge to postpone the trial for murder until they could approach a witness who had been sharing a cell with Owen. The judge agreed, and the case was put back until the next assizes.

At the second trial, the three boatmen, James Owen, George Thomas (sometimes known as Dobell) and William Ellis (sometimes known as Lambert), were jointly charged with the murder of Christina Collins by casting her into the canal, causing her to drown. William Brookes gave evidence of what he had heard and seen at Stoke-on-Trent, where Mrs Collins had complained about the men's behaviour. Brookes said that it was his opinion that the crew had been helping themselves to the spirits in the boat's cargo. He recalled hearing Christina say to Thomas, 'Leave me alone. I'll not have anything to do with you.' Brookes stated that Thomas had replied in foul and abusive language.

Hugh Cordwell, a Trent and Mersey Canal Company check clerk based at Stone, told the court that when Christina had informed him of her fear of the crew, he had noted that the captain, James Owen, was particularly drunk. John Tansley, an assistant clerk to the Canal Company, said that Christina Collins had arrived at Aston Lock on foot, walking along the towpath. Owen's boat arrived a little later at about 8.30 pm and Christina had rejoined it. He had heard one of the crew verbally abuse her and had seen Owen offer her a drink, which she refused.

Thomas Blore, captain of another Pickford's boat, gave evidence that he had exchanged words with Owen when their boats passed at about 9 pm on the Saturday night. Owen had been very crude about his female passenger, saying that if he didn't get his way with her he would 'burke' her. Blore said that he took this to be a reference to Burke and Hare, who would kill their victims, then sell their bodies for medical research.

A second canal boat captain, Robert Walker, informed the court that, shortly after seeing a woman walking along the towpath, he had met Owen's boat. One of the crew, he was unsure which, had asked him if he'd seen a woman walking by the canal, and again described in vulgar detail what he would like to do to her. This had occurred at about 10 o'clock.

The willingness of many of these witnesses to give evidence against fellow boatmen may well have been due to their underlying feelings of guilt. They had ignored Christina Collins' frequent appeals for help, or simply advised her to complain at the end of her journey. They must have seen the distress she was in and they could have given her more assistance, though of course they couldn't have guessed how far matters would eventually go.

James Mills stated that he and his wife Anne were asleep at Hoo Mill Lock on the night in question. They were woken by screams at midnight, and looking out had seen the three men by the boat and a woman sitting on the cabin roof shouting. Mills said that his wife had asked the men who the woman was, and had been told that she was a passenger and that her husband was accompanying her.

John Lee said that when Owen's boat reached Woodend Lock, near King's Bromley, early on Monday morning, the captain had reported that a 'deranged' woman passenger had drowned herself. Lee added that Owen was drunk and shaking. However, John Bladon, an employee of the Trent and Mersey Canal Company, told the court that Owen had not reported the loss of his passenger when the boat had passed through Rugeley, as would have been his duty under company rules.

Evidence was given by Samuel Barratt, a local surgeon, that he had examined Christina's body at the Talbot Inn, Rugeley, and had concluded that death was due to suffocation and drowning. He had noted two bruises on her right arm. Hannah Phillips and Elizabeth Matthews stated that they had removed the clothes from the dead woman. They had noticed that her calico drawers were ripped across the front, and one sleeve and cuff of Christina's gown were also torn.

Robert Collins, the husband of the victim, gave his evidence in tears, telling how he had identified his wife's body by a birthmark on her ear.

James Orgill said that he had shared a cell with Owen in Stafford gaol, and the captain had told him that it was Thomas and Ellis who had killed Christina Collins. Musson, the boy member of the crew, told the court that he had been in bed at the time of the murder, and he had heard Ellis snoring. Neither of these witnesses made much impression on the jury however, and a verdict of guilty was pronounced against all three men.

Extract from a pamphlet on the trial and execution of the two boatmen.
(Staffordshire Police Museum)

The judge, Mr Baron Gurney, sentenced the three men to death by hanging, saying that the case was one of the most shocking he had ever heard. A helpless and unoffending woman had been under their protection but had first been the object of their lust, then, to avoid detection, the object of their cruelty. He advised them not to look for pardon in this world, but to prepare themselves for an ignominious death.

An appeal on behalf of William Ellis was presented to the Secretary of State, pointing out that the evidence showed him to be less involved in the crime than his companions. As a result, the death sentence in his case was commuted to transportation for life, this news being given to him as the three condemned men were taking their final Sacrament from the prison chaplain. Then, as a result of a report from the governor of Stafford prison, the sentence against Ellis was further reduced from life to fourteen years and he was transported to Australia.

Owen and Thomas paid the ultimate price for the murder, and were hanged in front of Stafford gaol on 11th April 1840. Ten thousand spectators attended the event, many regarding it as an exciting day's entertainment, especially when accompanied by much drinking and merry-making. As was common at such public hangings, the local pickpockets made the most of the opportunity, despite the fact that theft was itself a hanging offence. It is also a fact that a public hanging always led to the local 'ladies of the night' doing a roaring trade. Why the men who had just watched their fellow-men die an unpleasant death on the gallows should be so aroused by it is something of a mystery!

The hangman was William Calcraft, who made a good living by travelling the country, conducting provincial hangings at £10 a time. His assistant should have been Tom Cheshire but Tom spent the night before drinking at the Shoulder of Mutton, and was so hung-over that he failed to turn up. The hangman needed an assistant, because the drop at that time was a short one, not sufficient to break the condemned man's neck. It was the assistant's task to go below the staging and hasten death by pulling on the hanged man's legs. Calcraft appealed to the governor of the prison, and a prisoner was found willing to escape his punishment by taking up a new career. George Smith became the hangman's assistant, and learned his trade so well that he eventually became a hangman in his own right, officiating at the execution of the notorious Dr William Palmer (see 'Saintly Billy').

THE ABBOTS BROMLEY HORN DANCE

❂

Once referred to as 'a pretty little town' and 'an inaccessible old township', Abbots Bromley is today definitely a village. It is famous as a result of a ritual that takes place there every September.

The annual Horn Dance is so old that its origins are lost in the mists of early history. It was described by Robert Plot in 1686, in his *Natural History of Staffordshire*, but the dance was almost certainly ancient even then. The six pairs of reindeer antlers used in the dance were always said to be of native British origin, which meant that they must date from before the 12th century when the native reindeer became extinct. Although most people wanted this to be true, it was regarded by cynics as just one of those folk myths, but what had been merely a theory was proved in 1976 to be true. A small sliver of bone from a broken horn tip was examined in the department of Geological Sciences at Birmingham University. A carbon dating procedure confirmed the antler as dating from around 1065, the year before the Battle of Hastings! It was not a myth after all.

The history of the horns of Abbots Bromley became confused at one time owing to the fact that six elk heads with horns were brought back from Turkey in 1703. These hung in the town hall for many years, until they were lost. This means that for a period there were six elk horns hanging in the town hall and six reindeer horns hanging in the church. It is unlikely that the much heavier elk horns

The Abbots Bromley horn dance in 2004.

were ever used in the dance, but there is a legend that both sets of horns – elk and reindeer – were taken to Burton-upon-Trent by the Abbots Bromley dancers, and the men became so inebriated that they left the elk horns behind! Fortunately the reindeer antlers were brought safely back to Abbots Bromley.

The reindeer antlers are still kept in the village church, which, it is delightful to note, is dedicated to Saint Nicholas, who in his guise as Santa Claus does have a strong association with reindeer.

Despite the church connection, the nature of the dance suggests that it pre-dates Christianity, and was originally a magic rite associated with hunting and fertility. The Church today accepts the Horn Dance but it would not always have been so accommodating. Theodore, the 7th-century Archbishop of Canterbury, banned 'the going about as a stag, or putting on the head or horns of beasts ... for this is devilish.'

The antlers have long been the subject of dispute between the church and the village. In her 1939 book on Abbots Bromley, Marcia Alice Rice, headmistress of the local girls' school from 1900–1933, comments that villagers are proud that the antlers have hung in the church for generations but that 'they are at once roused to anger if any vicar ventures to act regarding them without the consent of the dancers.' She quotes an incident in the late 19th century when there was unpleasantness between the vicar and the dancers over whether they could fetch the horns out of the church for a dance. When the vicar refused, the villagers held a meeting and it was the churchwarden not the vicar who eventually granted permission. In view of this, it may be significant that in 1981 the Abbots Bromley parish council formally took over the legal ownership of the antlers, though they still hang in church.

In might be thought that keeping the antlers in the village church might tame their older pagan spirit. This was not the experience of 27-year-old Jacky Ayre who visited Abbots Bromley with her parents in June 1988. Her father was keen to see the antlers, but the church door seemed to be locked. However, when they made enquiries, they were told that this could not be; the church was definitely open. They went back and tried again and found that this time the door opened easily.

Once inside, Jacky's parents went straight over to view the antlers but Jacky was amazed to find herself transfixed. In her own words, 'I couldn't move without great effort, and felt very strange and uneasy. The feeling grew to intense discomfort.' Forcing herself to move, Jacky left the church and immediately felt better. She decided to walk round the outside of the church, but encountered a pocket of freezing cold air. Again she was most surprised; it was a hot summer day, and everywhere else the temperature was in the high 70s.

A few years later, Jacky and her parents returned to Abbots Bromley, this time to watch the famous Horn Dance. Jacky decided to take the opportunity to check out her previous experience. She went back to the church, which this time – on the day of the Horn Dance – was packed with visitors. Jacky writes, '... but I felt the same horrible feelings as before, and again I had to leave.' She has no idea why this should have happened to her, and has so far been unable to discover whether other people have experienced the same thing. Could it be that the ritual of this ancient dance has maintained its power down the centuries and has an aura or a resonance that some people can feel?

The dance now takes place on 'Wakes Monday', early in September, also known as St Bartholomew's Day. Technically the date is calculated as being the Monday following the first Sunday after 4th September. However, when Robert Plot described it in the 17th century, it was performed around Christmas, namely on New Year's Day and Twelfth Night (6th January). This leads some scholars to believe that it was originally a winter solstice custom. The Abbots Bromley horn dancers take part in other festivals and events during the year, but when dancing away from the village, replica antlers are used.

Twelve men perform the Horn Dance. Six of them are the horn bearers and carry the antlers, which are mounted on wooden deer-heads carved in the 16th century. The largest set of antlers has a span of 39 inches and weighs over 25 pounds; the others are slightly smaller, the lightest weighing 16^1/$_2$ pounds. Three of the heads are painted white and three black, although in Robert Plot's day they were white and red.

The other performers are a Fool, a hobbyhorse, a boy with a bow and arrow (commonly referred to as Robin Hood), a man in woman's clothes and known as 'Maid Marian', a boy with a triangle and a musician with an accordion. Earlier musicians have played the violin, and before that the pipe and tabor. 'Maid Marian' wears a white veil and a dress reaching to the ground. She carries a stick and a wooden ladle in which she collects money. This man-dressed-as-woman character is known to pre-date the stories of Robin Hood's Maid Marian by many centuries.

Originally, the dancers wore their own clothes, decorated with ribbons, but in 1887 the wife of the Rev John Manley Lowe, the vicar of Abbots Bromley, designed a costume of knee breeches, knitted green stockings and sleeveless jerkins of red, brown and gold to make it look more medieval. The vicar's daughters, together with a Mrs Brown, utilised the old bed curtains from the vicarage to make the outfits. The costumes have had several changes since, and today they wear green breeches decorated with an oak leaf design, green and brown tunics and brown berets. The Fool, not surprisingly, wears a jester's motley, and the accordionist wears a wonderful hat decorated with long feathers.

On Wakes Monday, after a 7am service in the church, the antlers are taken outside and the first dance of the day is performed on the village green. This dance is performed for the vicar, and it is interesting to note that in this performance the Fool and the Maid Marian do not take part. Perhaps they are too irreverent for the church.

The next three dances take place in Abbots Bromley, at Goose Lane, then at two village farms. The twelve performers then set out on a 20-mile tour of the parish, taking in Blithfield Hall, the home of Lady Bagot, the lawn of a modern bungalow, humble cottages and outlying farms. At one time all the performers and followers would walk to all the locations but today a van transports the dancers to the places outside the village. It is widely believed that it would be bad luck to miss out any of the usual dancing places. The final dance is performed back in the village street, and the horns are returned to the church at 8.15 pm. For the performers, it has been a long and exhausting day. When the dancing is over, an evening of drinking and revelry begins. Perhaps the real pagan tradition of the original Horn Dance is recreated here!

At each of the seventeen locations, the same set dance is performed. It begins with a single file of dancers who form a circle, which loops into a figure of eight. Then on the leader's command, the horn bearers turn to face each other, the boy with the bow facing the hobbyhorse, and Maid Marian facing the Fool. They advance and retreat several times. Then the horn dancers pass their opposite number, shoulder to shoulder, one set holding their antlers up high so the horns do not tangle. This continues until the leader signals for the whole troupe to move on in procession.

In an article written in *Antiquities* in 1933, Violet Alford described the Abbots Bromley Horn Dance as 'the most primitive dance in Europe'. I think she was referring to the age of the dance, rather than the style of performance. The music is played by the accordionist, the beat emphasised by the boy playing his triangle, Maid Marian beating her stick and ladle together, the hobbyhorse snapping his jaws, and the boy with the bow clapping his bow and arrow. In her book *Abbots Bromley*, Marcia Alice Rice describes four old tunes that were used, including one known as 'Wheelwright Robinson's tune', but today some of the melodies seem comparatively modern. When I heard them, I'm sure I noticed the Lonnie Donegan tune 'Putting on the style', but this may have been played between the dances while the performers were relaxing with a drink. In the 1930s, people were grumbling about hearing the tune 'Yankee Doodle'. I think it fair to say that, in terms of the music, the Horn Dance is a growing and changing event, combining the contemporary with the traditional.

For many years, the dances were performed by two local families, the Fowells and the Bentleys, and it was interesting that in September 2004 there were three generations of Fowells taking part. Watching some of the dances that year, I was fascinated to see that the dancers were not at all possessive about their roles. At several locations, the first dance was performed by the official dancers, but then a few of them would drop out for the second performance. Spectators – male and female – were allowed to join in this time, even carrying the precious horns. The real dancers returned for the final performance before the whole troupe moved on.

Among the spectators, I spoke to George Jones who was collecting donations from the onlookers. He told me that he had taken part in the Horn Dance for nearly thirty years until problems with his knee ruled out dancing this year. Starting out as a relief dancer, filling in when a dancer was unavailable, he then had different roles, ultimately spending 20 years as the hobbyhorse. 'You don't have to be a Fowell or a Bentley, then?' I asked him. 'No, you don't,' he told me, adding, 'although I was married to a Fowell sister at one time.' He then said how glad he was that his divorce did not rule him out as a dancer! George introduced me to Terry Bailey, who has danced as the Fool since 1972. Another man who came into the dance as an outsider was Jack Brown, a Shropshire-born morris dancer. He was introduced into the Abbots Bromley dance in 1955 by Jim Fowell. In Jack's booklet *The Abbots Bromley Horn Dance*, he describes how Jim got over the problem of introducing a foreigner into the group by telling the locals that Jack was in fact John Tregorran, who was at that time a character in the radio serial *The Archers*. As such, he was accepted and allowed to dance as Maid Marian, but later took on other parts as well.

In 1686, when Dr Robert Plot wrote about the dance, he referred to the village as Pagets Bromley, since Henry VIII's dissolution of Burton Abbey had passed the ownership of the village to the Paget family. Dr Plot writes: '*At Abbots, or now rather Pagets Bromley, they had within living memory, a sort of sport, which they celebrated at Christmas (on New Year, and Twelft-day) call'd the Hobby-horse dance, from a person that carried the image of a horse between his leggs, made of thin boards, and in his hand a bow and arrow, which passing through a hole in the bow, and stopping upon a sholder it had in it, he made a snapping noise as he drew it to and fro, keeping time with the Musick; with this man danced 6 others, carrying on their shoulders as many Rain deers heads, 3 of them painted white, and 3 red, with the arms of the chief families (viz. Of Paget, Bagot, and Wells) to whom the revenews of the Town chiefly belonged, depicted on the palms of them, with which they danced the Hays, and other Country dances.*'

It is interesting to note that Plot calls it a 'Hobby-horse dance', with the horn dancers mentioned only as extras. Today, of course, it is named after the horn dancers, with the hobbyhorse and other characters being only part of the ritual. Also, in Plot's description the man dancing as the hobbyhorse carried the bow and arrow. He does not mention Robin Hood, the man-woman character or the Fool. Could these have been added later? Or perhaps these three characters may have been there in medieval times, disappeared for a while, then been reintroduced.

This leads us to consider just how old the dance is. The 1686 reference is certainly the earliest written account, and there are people who claim that it dates only from the 17th or possibly the 16th century. Another theory is that it dates from 1125 when the Abbot of Burton Abbey granted five men of Abbots Bromley grazing rights in Needwood Forest. Many, however, are convinced that it is even older, dating back to pre-Christian times.

Marcia Alice Rice takes Robert Plot to task for describing the Horn Dance as a sport. She writes: 'It is not now, and it never has been, a sport or a kind of amusement. No one who has seen the dance can think of it as anything but serious, whether deriving from pagan or Christian days. It is and always has been a rite. It is impersonal. It does not provoke amusement. It creates a sense of wonder and of respect.'

Jackie Barfoot, herself a pagan, recently wrote to me: 'I visited Abbots Bromley Horn Dance in 2002. To me it invoked the sprit of the horned God, the symbolism of the waning year, and the coming season of the rut and the hunt. I personally thought of it as a blessing to the spirit of Cerrinos or Herne, and as a blessing to make the forthcoming hunting season fruitful – also as a symbol of a fertility dance, imbuing the harvest and orchards with the spirit of the life force of the God and Goddess.'

The central part of the dance certainly shows the horn bearers charging and retreating, as if the reindeer were clashing their antlers during the rutting season. One ritual often missed by the spectators occurs at this point – the boy with the bow actually shoots the horse in the head, but the horse comes back to life, snaps his jaws and dances on. This is said to symbolise the ritual of death and rebirth.

Whether the dance is of Christian or pagan origins, it is a unique and awe-inspiring ritual to watch. It is one of Staffordshire's oldest and most famous mysteries.

WHO KILLED CARL BRIDGEWATER?

―――――――― ✿ ――――――――

Mary Poole and her cousin Fred Jones were retired farmers who lived at Yew Tree Farm in south-west Staffordshire with their land itself farmed by Hubert and Anthony Wilkes of the neighbouring Holloway Farm. The two cousins lived a very quiet life, with few visitors except for the local GP, Dr Angus Macdonald, and a boy, 13-year-old Carl Bridgewater, who delivered the local evening newspaper.

On Tuesday, 19th September 1978, Dr Macdonald thought he'd call at Yew Tree Farm to see Mary Poole, who'd been in hospital recently. He noticed the evening paper in the box by the door, and was alarmed to see that the wood around the lock on the door had been chipped away. The doctor went into the house and found Carl Bridgewater's body slumped on the settee in the living room.

Dr Macdonald drove to his own home and rang Kinver police station. PC Michael Fallon took the call at 5.30 pm, and was at the farm seven minutes later. Dr Macdonald returned to the farm, and followed the policeman into the house. He inspected the boy's body, and pronounced him dead.

PC Fallon saw that a ground-floor window at the front of the farmhouse was open, and the floor was covered in glass. He looked upstairs to ascertain that no one else was on the premises, then radioed for help. Two other officers from Kinver arrived, and together they discovered that the whole house had been ransacked. They fastened the back door and waited outside for the arrival of senior officers from Wombourne and Stafford, 9 miles and 30 miles away respectively. Detective Chief Superintendent Robert Stewart, head of Staffordshire CID, arrived and took charge.

At 7.30 pm, Fred Jones and Mary Poole returned home in a car driven by a friend, who had taken them out for the day. On arrival, they were shocked to find the farm drive full of police cars. After the police had told Mary and Fred what had happened, Dr Macdonald took the two shaken cousins to his own home for the night.

At 9 pm, Dr Benjamin Davies, a Home Office pathologist, arrived to take samples from the body and from the location. At 10 pm, the boy's body was removed to the mortuary at Wordsley hospital, where it was identified by Brian Bridgewater as that of his son Carl. Dr Davies discovered that Carl had been shot through the left side of the head by a single bullet from a shotgun from a distance of less than 4 feet.

When the police spoke to Fred Jones, he confirmed that the house at Yew Tree Farm was full of valuable antiques, but told the police that he could not think of any occasion when strangers had been in the house. Then he remembered a series of mystery phone calls, beginning in November 1977. The phone would ring, he would answer it, but there was never anyone there. Fred said that £70 had disappeared in April 1978 from an envelope at the bottom of a drawer in his bedroom. He also recalled that a few weeks previously, he had gone to Birmingham with Mary, leaving the door key under a slate on the coalhouse window ledge. On his return, Fred found the key lying in a different position. He fitted another lock, but said nothing about the missing money to Mary. Other things had gone missing in August and September, including a scythe from the garden, and an axe from the scullery. Fred asked Anthony Wilkes if he had borrowed them, but he had not.

The police noted that Fred's dog, Skip, had been left in the kitchen when the cousins left home that morning but was found by the police officers in the scullery. This raised the question of whether the intruder might have been someone the dog knew. Had some local person been keeping the house under scrutiny, making the mystery phone calls to find out if Fred and Mary were at home? The earlier robbery of £70 had occurred on the only other occasion when the cousins were both away. Chief Supt Bob Stewart was quoted in the *Express & Star* as saying, 'I tend to go for the view that the motive was that he [Carl Bridgewater] could have recognised his assailant.'

Outside in the yard and orchard, the police found a quite a few items that had been taken from the house and then abandoned, including a brooch and a silver teapot. Fingerprints, which did not belong to Fred or Mary, were found on several of these, and on Carl Bridgewater's yellow bike, unearthed in the farm pigsty.

Among the objects still missing were a copper kettle, a copper warming pan, two brass meat jacks, two brass candlesticks, an oak tantalus with three cut-glass decanters, a lady's pocket watch, a heavy silver watch chain, and two pairs of gold and silver cufflinks. These had been taken from all over the house: the sitting room, hall, billiard room and various bedrooms. The list of stolen items was distributed to the press.

Gladys Jones, whose garden overlooked Yew Tree Farm, told the police that, at 4 pm on the day of the murder, she saw a light blue car, probably a Ford Cortina estate, parked in the gateway of Yew Tree Farm, with its boot lifted. The back door of the farm was closed, indicating to her that Fred and Mary were out. Gladys walked into the field for a closer look, and saw that the back door was now open. She took another look at the farmhouse at 4.30 pm and noted that the car had gone, but the back door of the farmhouse was still open. She recalled that at no time had she heard Skip barking, as he always did at strangers.

Yew Tree Farm, where Carl was murdered. (Wolverhampton Express & Star)

The next day, the police commenced house-to-house inquiries in the area. Fourteen people said that they had seen a car on the farm driveway between 12.25 pm and 5 pm on the afternoon of the murder. Six thought it was a saloon, four were certain it was an estate, two said it was a van and the remaining two were unsure. All shades of blue were mentioned from light, through medium to dark. Only four had seen anyone in or near the vehicles. These included company director Roger Edwards, who was driving along Lawnswood Road at 2.50 pm and saw a pale blue Vauxhall Viva turn into the farm drive. He said that the driver was a man of about 55, with wavy hair that was dark but slightly greying. The man was wearing a dark blue uniform and Mr Edwards had the impression that he was a police officer or a fireman.

Terry Phelps, a builder, had driven past Yew Tree Farm at around 5 pm and had seen a dark blue vehicle parked in the drive, with either two or three men in it. The car was facing him, and Terry saw that the driver was a dark-haired man in his late forties, wearing a light shirt and a tie.

Another witness, restaurant manager Mario Sabetta, stated that he had seen a blue vehicle parked on the main A449, about a hundred yards from the farm, at 3.25 pm. He saw two men, one in his late twenties with fair shoulder-length curly hair, the other a slim, dark-haired man in his late thirties. The younger man was carrying a shotgun, and Mr Sabetta had assumed they were going rabbiting.

By now, the police were working on the theory that there were three men involved in the robbery and murder. An Identikit picture of the man seen by Terry Phelps was released by the police and published in the press on 29th September. Seven hundred calls were received at Wombourne police station from members of the public who thought they recognised the face. Each call had to be followed up and investigated. Two more Identikit pictures, this time based on Mario Sabetta's sighting, were released to the press and brought a new series of phone calls from the public. The owners of 7,000 blue Cortina estates were questioned. By mid-November, 5,000 statements had been taken, and 7,500 phone calls received.

At this stage, the investigating officers returned to the statement of Roger Edwards, who had seen the uniformed man in a Vauxhall Viva. The two officers who had taken Mr Edward's original statement were told to trace the Viva and its owner. They visited every police station, fire station and ambulance station in the area, followed by depots belonging to the water board, gas board, electricity board, post office and even the RSPCA. At each, they asked about any uniformed men who drove a blue Vauxhall Viva. Eventually they came up with the name of Bert Spencer, an ambulance driver based at Corbett Hospital, Stourbridge.

When interviewed, Spencer said that on the afternoon of the murder, he had been on duty at the hospital until 5 pm. A neighbour, Mrs Barbara Riebold, who worked as an ambulance secretary at the same hospital, confirmed this. Nevertheless, police interest in Bert Spencer increased when they learned that his name had been given to them earlier in the investigation as a man who bought and sold antiques. At his interview, Spencer said that he was a collector of antiques, but not a dealer. However, this was soon proved incorrect.

He also had several connections with Carl Bridgewater and Yew Tree Farm. He knew the farmhouse and its owners well, frequently borrowing a shotgun to go rabbiting, and he had been inside the farmhouse on many occasions. He knew, and was known by, Skip the dog. Between 1970 and 1975, Bert Spencer had lived in Wordsley, where he was a close neighbour of the Bridgewater family. The police were also interested in the fact that Spencer often drove past Yew Tree Farm on his way to and from work.

When re-interviewed by DCI Weslea Watson and DS Tony Holdway, Bert Spencer admitted that he often worked for Mr Wilkes, doing part-time farmwork at Yew Tree Farm. He was asked why he had failed to mention this before, and replied that he didn't want his employers in the ambulance service to find out about his farmwork. Asked about visiting the farmhouse, Spencer said that he had been there 'hundreds of times'. He agreed that he had been there in uniform but, when asked whether he could have visited Yew Tree Farm on the day of the murder, Spencer replied, 'I would say I wasn't in Lawnswood Road that day.'

However, police interest in Bert Spencer faded when on Friday, 30th November, an isolated farmhouse in Worcestershire was robbed. Two masked men, one of whom was armed with a sawn-off shotgun, broke into Chapel Farm, Romsley, and demanded money from the elderly family who lived there. They stole £200, and made their getaway in a green Austin 1100 driven by a third man. As the raiders ran to the car and drove off, a window cleaner noted the car's registration number.

The similarities between this robbery and the robbery and murder at Yew Tree Farm struck the police immediately: an isolated farmhouse, elderly occupants, three robbers and a shotgun. Surely, these were no mere coincidences. The car registration was traced to a Linda Galvin of Northfields, Birmingham, and when the police visited her they discovered that 25-year-old Vincent Hickey had been living with her since August. Vincent was serving a suspended sentence for deception linked to a robbery in Hertfordshire, and he was a member of a close-knit family with links to the Birmingham underworld. He had already been questioned in the Carl Bridgewater case because he had once owned a blue Cortina estate. All other lines of investigation were dropped as the police began a hunt for Vincent Hickey.

For the previous three years, Vincent had been working as an itinerant roofer with three of his cousins, cold-calling on house owners all over the country, suggesting that their roofs needed attention. When an elderly man in Rickmansworth allowed them to repair his roof, he paid them from a bag which clearly contained a great deal of money. The four roofers decided to steal it. When the robbery took place, Vincent made sure that he and his 15-year-old cousin, Michael, had an established alibi elsewhere. But, when a piece of headed notepaper left at the house was traced back to Vincent, he'd offered to give the names of his accomplices so long as the police charged him with deception and not robbery. When the case came to trial, he received a suspended two-year sentence, though one of his cousins had received four years in prison. The 'moral' was not lost on Vincent: it paid to inform!

Vincent had taken part in a different scam in September. He learned that the elderly resident of Chapel Farm in Worcestershire always paid for his coal from a tin full of cash. He and Linda Galvin had driven out to the farm, where Linda had introduced herself as the coal merchant's daughter. She said that the residents could save money by paying for their winter coal in advance, and coolly accepted a payment of £350. As the swindlers drove away, Vincent was very much aware that there was still money left in the old man's tin. He again recruited his young cousin, Michael, and another acquaintance, 44-year-old Jimmy Robinson and, together, they raided Chapel Farm. But the robbery did not go well: they got away with only £200, they met a spirited resistance from the occupants, and their car registration was noted.

On 1st December, the police called again on Linda Galvin. As she went to open the door, Vincent Hickey slipped out of the back bedroom window. He spent the next few days hiding, but when he heard that the police were linking the Chapel Farm robbery with the Carl Bridgewater killing, he went into Bromsgrove police station and gave himself up.

Vincent was questioned by officers of various police forces, including detectives from Staffordshire. He stated that his cousin Michael had taken part in the robbery at Chapel Farm with two other men, his own involvement being restricted to lending them the car. He began to mention other robberies the men had committed, before throwing in the bombshell remark, 'Our Michael says the older one did the Bridgewater murder!' Two days later, he named the man as Jimmy Robinson. Further questioned about the murder, Vincent Hickey also gave the police the name of Pat Molloy.

The police were quite excited by this information. Robinson was known to them and had served a suspended sentence for involvement in a robbery at Tamworth, and Molloy was his frequent drinking companion. When Robinson went into Harbourne Lane police station on 6th December to report for bail, he was arrested and charged with the Chapel Farm robbery. In the early hours of the next day, Jimmy Robinson admitted his part in the raid, and took the police to where his shotgun and eleven cartridges were hidden. He still denied any connection with the Yew Tree Farm killing. Pat Molloy, a 50-year-old carpenter, was arrested on 8th December and charged with involvement in the Tamworth robbery. The police continued to seek Michael Hickey.

The three men in custody, Vincent Hickey, Jimmy Robinson and Pat Molloy, were questioned at length over the next few days, with 38 separate interviews taking place between 7th and 10th December. Unfortunately, these occurred before the routine tape-recording of interviews became a legal requirement, and the police notes were made after, rather than during, the interviews. There were no solicitors present, and the three suspects were held in solitary confinement when not being questioned.

Vincent Hickey continually asked for bail in return for the help he was giving. He continued to say that he 'had a feeling' that Robinson and Molloy were involved in the killing of Carl Bridgewater. Throughout sixteen hours of questioning, Vincent continued to tease the police with small snippets of information, even saying at one time that he had been present at Yew Tree Farm, but he refused to sign any written statement. Jimmy Robinson never wavered in his denial of any involvement in the killing of the newspaper boy.

Pat Molloy was a different type of man, older, nervous and anxious to please. After three days of questioning, he finally agreed that he had been there with the Hickey cousins and Jimmy Robinson. Molloy said that he was upstairs, searching for money in a bedroom, when he heard the sound of the gunshot. He said that when he went downstairs, he saw the boy's body, and was told by Jimmy Robinson that the gun had gone off accidentally. To the intense relief of the police, Pat Molloy signed this statement. However, he later amended his version of events to say that, when he came downstairs after the gunshot, only the Hickey cousins were there, Michael holding the gun. He thought that Jimmy Robinson must have been upstairs.

Molloy was actually taken by the police to Yew Tree Farm, but failed to recognise the location. There were also several anomalies in his statement – he was extremely vague about the details and he made no mention of the dog at the farm. Nevertheless, the police hoped that when they knew of Molloy's statement, Vincent Hickey and Jimmy Robinson would break down and confess. However, both men dismissed it as a pack of lies, and the police realised that they would need to rely on Molloy's very confused and contradictory statement to make their case at a trial.

When Michael Hickey, now aged sixteen, was arrested on 20th December, he immediately confessed to taking part in the Chapel Farm raid and another robbery at a Tesco store, but denied that he had anything to do with the events at Yew Tree Farm. He maintained this throughout three interviews on 21st December and a further five on the 22nd. DI Watson returned to Pat Molloy and questioned him about his two versions of who had the gun when it was fired: Molloy now said that he didn't know which account was the correct one.

All four men were charged with murder and appeared at Stafford Crown Court in October 1979. Mr Justice Drake ruled that no evidence relating to the Chapel Farm robbery was to be introduced, as it would prejudice the murder case. Ironically, this ruling in favour of the defence was later to hamper the evidence given by Vincent Hickey. He was unable to explain to the jury why he had attempted to offer the police snippets of information about the Carl Bridgewater case in an attempt to buy sympathetic treatment in the case of earlier robbery.

The prosecution counsel, Philip Cox QC, told the jury that he would establish that a blue Cortina estate car and a Transit-type van were at Yew Tree Farm between 3.45 pm and 4.45 pm on the afternoon of the murder. Because police inquiries had established that the four defendants had

Michael Hickey in 1979. (Wolverhampton Express & Star)

cast-iron alibis for the period before 3 pm on the afternoon of the murder, the prosecution called only those witnesses who had seen vehicles at Yew Tree Farm after 3.25 pm. Thus, the jury did not hear from several witnesses, including Roger Edwards who had seen a Vauxhall Viva being driven by a man in uniform at 2.50 pm.

Those witnesses who were called, including the neighbour Gladys Jones, gave evidence that they had seen a blue estate car. This was important to the prosecution case, as Vincent Hickey had once owned a car of this type. However, the defence was able to prove that his car had been written-off after an accident in 1977 when he collided with a car driven by an off-duty policewoman.

Although Vincent Hickey had, on legal advice, refused to take part in any identification parade, his cousin Michael had been very willing to do so, until his solicitor realised that his client was to be the only man in the line-up with a beard. Pat Molloy did take part in an ID parade, but none of the eight witnesses picked him out.

The identification evidence in the case of Jimmy Robinson was more complicated. None of the eight witnesses picked him out at the actual parade, but three of them later told the police that Robinson was the nearest in appearance to the man they had seen near Yew Tree Farm. However, defence counsel was able to point out that all the witnesses had described a man with collar-length hair, whereas his client had actually shaved his head completely on 25th August and his hair could not have grown very much by 19th September.

The prosecution brought forward evidence that Robinson had bought a shotgun in September, and the gun had been used in robberies since that time. Soon after his arrest, Robinson had admitted this, and had taken the police to where his gun and cartridges were hidden. Robinson's gun was produced in court. A ballistics expert testified that shotguns did not leave identifiable markings on a bullet and that it was therefore impossible to say whether Robinson's shotgun was the one used to kill Carl Bridgewater. He did add that the cartridges found with Robinson's gun were not of the type used to kill Carl.

Vincent and Michael Hickey both had witnesses who had seen them drinking in the Dog and Partridge pub until 3 pm, and claimed that at 4.30 pm they had been at a garage looking at cars. Jimmy Robinson's alibi was that he and Pat Molloy had been drinking at the California pub until lunchtime, and had then gone to the home of his girlfriend where they had had some dinner, before falling asleep. Pat Molloy, who had withdrawn his confession three days after making it, now confirmed Robinson's version of events.

In court, Molloy was faced with a dilemma. He could claim that his statement was false and made under duress, and risk the jury concluding that they could believe nothing he said, or he could allow his statement to stand. After all, it did put him upstairs at the time of the killing. In the event, Molloy decided that although he was pleading not guilty, he would not challenge the statement.

His counsel announced, 'My Lord, we call no evidence on behalf of Molloy.' This was a turning point in the trial. Although the law held that Molloy's statement was not evidence against anyone except himself – and the judge was meticulous in explaining this legal point to the jury – its influence was considerable.

The jury brought in verdicts of guilty of murder against Jimmy Robinson, Vincent Hickey and Michael Hickey. Pat Molloy was found guilty of manslaughter. Jimmy Robinson and Vincent Hickey were sentenced to life imprisonment, with a recommendation that each serve 25 years. Pat Molloy was sentenced to twelve years. And Michael Hickey, who was fifteen at the time of the killing, was to be detained at Her Majesty's Pleasure.

However, the case of the Bridgewater Four as the convicted men came to be known – they became the Bridgewater Three when Pat Molloy died in 1981 – has been a controversial one ever since. None of the three has ever admitted his guilt, even though their life in prison would have been more comfortable if they had. Michael Hickey spent 89 days of the bitter winter of 1983-84 on the roof of Gartree Prison, protesting his innocence. The fact that his fellow prisoners supported him throughout this period does not prove his innocence, though it does indicate that the other prisoners believed him. The treatment of convicted child-killers by other prisoners is not normally very sympathetic.

A bizarre postscript to the case took place in 1980 when Bert Spencer, the ambulance driver interviewed by the police, was himself found guilty of a murder. A month after the end of the Bridgewater trial, Spencer shot dead Hubert Wilkes, the farmer who worked the land at Yew Tree Farm. Bert Spencer claimed that he had blacked out and could not recall the shooting, but he was found guilty of murder and sentenced to life imprisonment.

In October 1987, the then Home Secretary Douglas Hurd referred the Bridgewater case to the Court of Appeal, but the appeal was dismissed, and, for the next nine years, all calls for a reopening of the case of the convicted men were turned down. Television programmes were made, books written, MPs on both sides of the House took up the cause, and some members of the original jury – including the foreman – have come out publicly to support the case for a new inquiry. One of the leading campaigners for the release of the men was the late Paul Foot, whose book *Murder at the Farm* revealed much of what had gone wrong with the handling of the case.

In 1996, Michael Chance, the official who had handled the prosecution for the Director of Public Prosecutions, stated that he thought it 'a disturbing error' that certain evidence, particularly the fact that the fingerprints found on Carl's bike did not match the prints of any of the accused, was not made available to the defence at the time of the trial. Mr Chance said that this caused him a great deal of concern and militated towards the Home Secretary giving further consideration to a new referral to the Court of Appeal. Following these comments, Michael Howard, Home Secretary at that time, announced in July 1996 that the case would be allowed to go to the Court of Appeal.

Michael Hickey protesting his innocence on the roof of Gartree Prison, Leicestershire, in January 1984. (Leicester Mercury)

The appeal was successful, the judges stated that the police officers' account of Pat Molloy's confession 'was most improbable, if not impossible'. Molloy had made his statement after having been shown an alleged confession by Michael Hickey. New evidence put before the court indicated that Hickey's signature was comparable with that of DC John Perkins, and that its wording was that of DC Graham Leeke. Lord Justice Roche stated that one of the officers, DC Perkins, 'was prepared to resort to deceit to obtain evidence'. They also found that the evidence against Michael Hickey was 'of such a tenuous character that a reasonable jury properly directed could not convict on it', and that in the case of Jimmy Robinson there were concerns about identification against him and the treatment of his alibi. The three surviving members of the Bridgewater Four were released, after spending eighteen years in prison.

Who killed Carl Bridgewater? The mystery may never be solved, as the police have no plans to re-open the case.

THE SARACENS OF BIDDULPH MOOR

———————— ❁ ————————

For many years there has been a strange belief that the people of Biddulph Moor, high up in north-west Staffordshire, were a unique race descended from Moors or Saracens. Not only did they have an uncommon appearance, swarthily handsome with piercing eyes, noses curved 'like a sword' and prominent cheekbones, but they also spoke a dialect so peculiar that it couldn't be understood even in the nearby towns of Biddulph or Leek. The people of the surrounding parts of Staffordshire often refer to them as 'the blacks o' Biddle Moower'. A BBC Radio 4 programme – broadcast in July 2003 – looked at this belief and the circumstances behind it. The programme, called *Meet The Descendants*, examined both oral and written evidence, as well as attempting to find scientific proof.

The legend tells that seven Saracens (though another source says twelve) were brought back to England as prisoners after the Crusades, by a nobleman called Orme of Biddulph, and these men intermarried with the local women to produce the present-day race of Biddulph Moor folk. In many versions, the Saracens were marvellous stonemasons who worked on the churches of St Chad's and St Mary's in Stafford, and St Lawrence's in Biddulph, before being abandoned to make their own life high up on the moorlands. It is certainly true that the people of Biddulph Moor have been skilled stonemasons for centuries, and the local surnames Stonier and Stanier are derived from the profession of Stonehewer.

In Stafford, thirty miles to the south, there is a strong belief that Saracen stonemasons were brought back by Orme from the Crusades to work on the churches of St Chad's and St Mary's, before being sent to live on Biddulph Moor. In the chancel of St Chad's, at the top of one of the columns is a Latin inscription that translates as 'He who built me is called Orme'. This does strongly indicate that Orme of Biddulph did build the church, but did he use Saracen masons? Much of the stonework seems to depict figures that are more exotic than Christian. One shows a human figure standing with arms outstretched, holding a tree and standing on an upturned human head. While some have seen this as David and Goliath, others reckon it to be a representation of the Babylonian fertility goddess Ishtar. The font in St Mary's church also has features that suggest influences from foreign parts. The images on the font are of human figures but underneath are lions and monkeys. The Latin inscription translates as 'You are not wise if you do not flee the lions'. A second inscription reads 'You bear from Jerusalem the water of the divine fountain which fills me with beauty and grace'. The representation of lions and monkeys in an English church is extremely unusual and may be unique. There are far fewer overtly Christian symbols than exotic ones, and many scholars believe that they do indicate the work of stonemasons from the Middle East.

A prominent family name in Biddulph Moor is that of the Baileys. One version of the legend has a member of the Saracen clan becoming the bailiff to Orme of Biddulph, and over the years the Bailiffs became the Baileys. Certainly the present Baileys – like most Biddulph Moor people – are very proud of their Saracen roots. John Bould, whom I met in Biddulph Library in November 2004, told me that his folk came from Biddulph Moor and that he likes to think that his ancestors were from a Saracen warrior race. An article in

Reveille published in 1966 quoted two local men, Leonard Brown and undertaker William Booth, both claiming to come of Saracen stock. Mr and Mrs Michael Biddulph from 'the big house' – they left Biddulph Old Hall in 1963 to go to live in Gloucestershire – say that they too are convinced of the Saracen ancestry story. However, they believe that the nobleman who brought the Saracens back from the Crusades was a later descendant of Orme named Thomas de Biddulph who lived in the 13th century, which would certainly tie in with the Crusades.

In 1978 new evidence was produced when Frederic Hails, the coroner for Stoke-on-Trent and District, stated: 'In the 19 years I have been here, I have seen a significant difference in the blood groups of the deceased from Biddulph Moor than in the rest of north Staffordshire. I have also heard this from the medical circles in which I work. There is speculation that this peculiar blood group is also found in Middle Eastern peoples, though that is not a matter of fact.'

In the BBC programme, DNA samples were taken from four members of the present-day Baileys of Biddulph Moor and these were sent to Dr Martin Richards of Huddersfield University. Dr Richards managed to extract DNA from three of the four samples, but the sequence he analysed was common to peoples from both Europe and the Middle East. The experiment was therefore inconclusive, and neither proved nor disproved the Saracen connection.

Written references to the Saracens of Biddulph Moor began much earlier than the 1966 article or the coroner's comments of 1978. The story of the Saracen ancestry was included in *Memorials of Old Staffordshire* edited by W. Beresford in 1909, where the children of Biddulph Moor are described as having 'the most lovely shades of red-gold hair'. It should be noted that other writers have included dark hair in their description of the Biddulph Moor folk.

In Sleigh's *A History of the Ancient Parish of Leek*, published in 1862, the author states that 'One of the lords of

Biddulph Castle, a knight crusader, is reputed to have brought over in his train from the Holy Land a Paynim who he made bailiff of his estate, and from his marriage with an English woman the present race of "Biddle-moor men" is traditionally said to have sprung. Probably this infusion of Saracenic blood may account for their nomadic and somewhat bellicose propensities.'

One man who thinks that the legend of Saracen ancestors may be mistaken is Reg Bowers of Mow Cop. When I went to see him, Reg told me that he considered it most unlikely that the Crusaders would have brought back any Saracen prisoners. 'Neither side took prisoners during the Crusades,' he argues, 'and I'm sure that the Church would not have employed Moslem Saracens to work as stonemasons, not in those days.' Reg Bowers' theory is that the men who were brought to Staffordshire at the time of the Crusades were in fact Falashas, the black Jews of Ethiopia. He points out that the carvings on the font in St Mary's church are of monkeys and lions, indicating African influence rather than that of the Middle East. Other people have wondered whether the ancestors may have actually been Gypsies, who were often referred to in previous centuries as 'Egyptians'.

Retired history teacher Arnold Gibson of Knypersley admits that he is a sceptic about the whole legend. 'It is easy to see how Biddulph Moor lent itself to the story of the Saracens,' he told me. 'It is moorland, poor farming land. Any lord of the manor would be glad to let it off at low rents, especially since it was even more remote and difficult to reach than Biddulph itself. So there grew up a community of small farmers, marrying within their own group – as all villagers did before the days of easy travel – but these were even more isolated, suspicious and resentful of strangers. They would speak their own dialect, one so strange and unintelligible to outsiders as to appear a foreign language. The tale of the Saracens could start from there.'

The Baileys and many other Biddulph Moor families, however, prefer to accept the traditional belief that they are genuinely descended from Saracens, and even the sceptical Arnold Gibson admits that it would be a pity to lose the stories.

One aspect of the mystery that none of the theories really explain is that of the red hair. The eyes, the noses, the dark complexions can be explained as Saracen, Ethiopian, or Gypsy in origin but Beresford's book does mention red-gold hair. This phenomenon was confirmed to me by John Bould who said that at school the Beech family were always known as 'reddies' because of their hair colour, though other families did have the dark hair that might have been expected from a Saracen bloodline.

The red hair remains a mystery within a mystery.

THE FAULD DISASTER

❁

The underground explosion that took place in November 1944, at an underground ammunition depot at Fauld gypsum mines near Hanbury, was the largest the UK has ever experienced. Worldwide, it was the largest explosion of the Second World War, apart from the two atom bombs on Hiroshima and Nagasaki, and it was heard in Leicester and Coventry, cities 70 miles away. It was even picked up on seismographic instruments in Geneva. The pilot of a plane flying over the Humber, 100 miles to the north-west, reported seeing the flash.

It was just after 11 am on a Monday morning, and John Cooper was a 9-year-old in the village school at the time. When the massive bang was heard, the whole school shook and the pupils were ordered to shelter under their desks. 'Sensible advice,' he told me, 'but we were young lads.' John and a few of his friends decided to leave the school and explore the village. They tried the front door but were driven back by slates and coving stones falling from the roof. Escaping via the back door, they made their way up the village in a state of shock at the damaged houses and the sight of general devastation. At the local pub, the Cock Inn, they discovered two large holes in the yard in front. These had been caused by falling rocks, and were rapidly filling up with water from a burst water main. About half a mile away, there was a huge mushroom cloud in the sky. This was before the atom bombs, and no one had seen anything like it. 'Most of the rocks and heavy stuff had come down in the first few minutes,' John recalls, 'but a huge cloud of dust came down in Hanbury and for miles around nearly three hours later at about 2 pm.'

The disused gypsum mines at Fauld had been acquired by the Air Ministry in 1937, as there was a growing need for storage space for ammunition. It seemed an ideal site. The mines lay 90 feet below Stonepit Hills, and there was enough capacity to store 10,000 tons of bombs. During the mining process, natural pillars of rock had been left to support the roof every 20 feet or so. To convert the mines into an explosive store, all that was needed was the provision of a concrete roof lining, and the building of two walls. One was an internal 10 feet thick wall sub-dividing the High Explosive store, and the other a much more substantial barrier, 50 feet thick, separating the HE store from the area where incendiaries were to be held.

A light railway was built to transport the explosive material from the main railway line at Scropton, about a mile away to the north. The light railway actually ran

The Peter Ford Works after the explosion. (John Cooper)

directly into the Fauld mine, and had branches and loops inside the mine leading into all the storage areas.

In 1941–2, it proved necessary to enlarge the storage area into unused parts of the mine to accommodate a further 10,000 tons of explosive, in effect doubling the capacity. There was a potential problem in that a working gypsum mine owned by Peter Ford Ltd, a manufacturer of plasterboard, was located close to the new storage area. However, all the experts were agreed that the wall of rock, varying between 15 and 50 feet in thickness, separating Ford's from the new store would provide a sufficient blast barrier. The light railway line was extended into the new area.

The whole operation was run by the RAF and was known as 21 MU, which stood for Maintenance Unit no 21. It was manned by 18 officers, 475 servicemen and 445 civilians. When, in late 1944, more manpower was needed, 195 Italians from a camp at Hilton were brought in. Although these Italians are almost always referred to as being prisoners-of-war, this is not technically correct, since Italy had already signed an armistice with the Allies. The men had formerly been prisoners-of-war but were now known as co-operators, and they were actually paid a wage for their work at 21 MU.

The disaster occurred at 11.10 am on Monday, 27th November. In fact, there was a double explosion: a sharp crack initially, followed seconds later by an unbelievable blast of catastrophic proportions. Three thousand tons of explosives detonated, taking off the roof of the mine-workings and also the 90 feet of earth and rock above it. Stonepit Hills erupted, hurling a million tons of earth and rocks into the air over the surrounding area. As the pieces of gypsum descended, and some of them weighed over 20 tons, Hanbury and its environs were subjected to a sudden bombardment. In Hanbury, few buildings were untouched, and the village hall and the Cock Inn were so badly damaged that they had to be rebuilt. In Burton-upon-Trent, five miles to the south-east, church steeples were severely cracked and 150 houses damaged. The dust, which it has been estimated had been thrown eleven miles into the sky, came down three hours later blocking out all light in Hanbury.

Upper Castle Hayes Farm had stood directly above the site of the explosion. Together with two adjacent woods, the farm disappeared completely. Hanbury Fields Farm, situated a quarter of a mile away, was first bombarded with rock, and then buried in falling earth and debris. John Cooper's mother was working at Hanbury Fields Farm. 'Being a Monday,' John told me, 'she was doing the washing, of course.' The farmer and his wife were away at market, but the farmer's mother was at home. John tells me that his mother grabbed the lady and pulled her under the sturdy wooden table. 'It was a miracle that they both survived,' he says, 'because everyone else there was killed.'

Not only did Mary Cooper survive. She later helped with the terrible job of laying out all the dead in the village schoolroom. Tragically, among those whose bodies she attended to was that of her own husband, John's father. Joseph Cooper had been driving a locomotive inside the mine at the time in question. In later years, John himself worked at the mine and he tells me that he even drove the same engine.

Mrs Cooper's work after the explosion did not go unnoticed. Early in 1945, John Auden, the coroner for East Staffordshire wrote, 'This woman, of her own free will, has cleaned and scrubbed a very gruesome temporary mortuary every day for 72 days. The work has been indescribable. She has helped with the undressing, and also with the washing of clothes removed from the bodies. One of the first victims that she had to deal with was her own husband. In most cases that would have been sufficient for a middle-aged woman to undertake without volunteering to continue the work with all the remainder. She survived the wrecking of a farm at which she was looking after an old lady, and it is

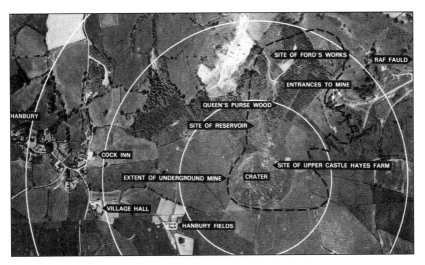

Aerial view of the site (circles are at ¹/₄ mile intervals).

probably due to her action that the old lady's life was saved.'

It was not just the volcano of rock and earth that caused loss of life. About 200 yards from the centre of the explosion there was a 30-foot dam, holding back a reservoir of water used in the production of plasterboard. The dam crumbled, sending a 15-foot torrent of water, mud, boulders and trees to pour down into the Ford's plasterworks, destroying the buildings and burying the workers there.

The crater that resulted from the Fauld explosion is about three-quarters of a mile long and half a mile wide. It is often said to be 120 feet deep, though John insists that the depth is more like 90 feet. 'The mine was 90 feet deep,' he explains, 'and the explosion simply took the top off it. I walked up to the crater with John recently and we looked down into it. It is certainly an impressive and awe-inspiring place. As we peered downwards, John pointed out the pieces of rock on the floor of the crater far below. He explained that they are in fact what is left of the natural gypsum pillars that once supported the roof of the mine workings.

The whole crater is securely fenced off and covered in notices warning visitors not to trespass because of the sudden drop and unexploded bombs. 'It's a bit ironic really, ' John commented. 'It wasn't fenced off until 1979. Before that, as young lads, we all played down there!' The whole area is surrounded by massive boulders of gypsum that fell from the sky that day, and John explained that what you can see is just the upper portion. Rather like icebergs, the part underground is even larger than the part seen above ground.

Up on the edge of the crater is a memorial to those, including Joseph Cooper, John's father, who lost their lives

The memorial at the edge of the crater.

on that terrible November day in 1944. The names include local farmworkers and mineworkers, as well as 33 RAF personnel. A number of the names are those of the Italian co-operators. Another is the name of a member of the mine rescue team, Jimmy Beard, who lost his life while working in the attempts to bring out any survivors.

It is said that 81 people died that day, though the memorial has only 70 names. Perhaps the exact figure will never be known for sure.

Bodies were still being found for several weeks, but some took much longer to be discovered. As the whole area was covered in more than three feet of debris, the fields were unusable. Prisoners from Sudbury Open Prison were brought in to slowly move the material. John tells me that two years after the explosion, a prisoner clearing the earth and debris hit something metal. He immediately stopped work and, as instructed, waved a red flag to attract his supervisor's attention. What he had found was a buried tractor, and beneath it was the body of the farmworker who had been driving it on the day the dump went up.

Not everyone in the mine perished, of course. RAF corporal Lionel Poynton crawled for an hour in complete darkness, covering three quarters of a mile by feeling his way along the railway and picking up other survivors as he went.

Immediately after the explosion, the attempts to find and rescue survivors began. The first people in were RAF men, accompanied by a civilian foreman, but they were hampered by not having lamps to light their way. They also met another hazard: carbon monoxide gas. The mine rescue team from Ashby was called in, and they brought a new professionalism – and specialised equipment – to the situation. Nevertheless, things were still very hazardous and Jimmy Beard died as a result of the fumes. Americans from their service hospital at Sudbury played their part in rescuing men from the Peter Ford works.

The disaster was reported locally and in the national press. The newspaper estimates of the number of deaths were very speculative and figures in excess of 200 were mentioned in the *Daily Mail*. This led to government criticism that the national papers were damaging public morale. The authorities would have preferred to keep all news of the Staffordshire disaster out of the public domain, and it soon became clear why. The Nazi propaganda machine seized on the event, and it was not long before Lord Haw-Haw was on German radio, claiming that it had been caused by sabotage. A few British people began to wonder whether the explosion might really have been set off by one of the Italian co-operators, or perhaps by the IRA. Other rumours at the time involved a bomb dropped from an enemy plane, or even a new radio-controlled V2 flying-bomb. These last two explanations were soon dismissed as impossible, and the coroner, after consulting with the Air Ministry, exonerated the Italian workers, bringing in a verdict of 'accidental death caused by an explosion on government property'.

In December 1944 Air Marshall Sir Graham Donald ordered a Court of Inquiry to be held to look into the events of 27th November, under the presidency of Air Vice Marshall A. Lees. To the annoyance of many, the findings of the Inquiry were only released to the public 30 years later, in November 1974. This delay in publishing the findings led to many conspiracy theories. What were the authorities trying to hush up, people asked. What were they hiding?

It is now known that the Inquiry was told that two aircraftsmen were working on a number of 1,000 pound medium case bombs. Normally this involved removing the nose and tail plugs, along with the exploder pocket which contained a primary charge of explosive. Where this proved impossible, the men would have to chisel out the composite explosive from the pocket and collect it in an ammunition box. The Inquiry concluded that the probable cause of the explosion was one of the men using an inappropriate brass chisel to chip out the primary charge from the bomb, which was one of many that had been sent to 21 MU as defective. The use of a brass chisel acting against the steel casing could have caused a spark, igniting the explosive. The bomb being worked on was one of a row, all of which were 'presumably exploded by sympathetic detonation or by fragments'. This in turn led to the whole of the material contained in the new area – over 3,500 tons of it – exploding.

The Court of Inquiry criticized the safety procedures in 21 MU, saying that although the regulations and standing orders were adequate, they were not being fully observed. It was also stated that the local relaxations in safety procedures may have led to familiarity breeding contempt. As a mitigating factor, the Inquiry commented that, during wartime, circumstances might exist 'where urgency is a keynote, manpower is of poorer quality and quantity, and more work is expected of a Unit than that for which it was designed.' The Air Ministry accepted responsibility for the accident and, on instructions from Winston Churchill, compensation was paid for both loss of life and damage to property.

So one man using a brass chisel instead of the more appropriate copper one seems to have been the cause of the terrible disaster. And yet it could have been even worse. The older and much larger ammunition store, which contained ten times more explosive and which was connected to the new area by a narrow tunnel, did not explode. If it had, then the loss of life would have been many times higher, and Burton-upon-Trent and much of east Staffordshire would have been wiped from the map of Britain.

John Cooper has no time for conspiracy theories, but something that irritates him is that statements are frequently made by politicians and bureaucrats that 'there may be unexploded material under the crater'. He knows that 'there may be' is the wrong phrase because the existence of such material is definite. He recently showed me a copy of an internal Air Ministry report from 1972, which states: 'The crater area and the majority of the area hatched blue have been searched and cleared to a depth of about eighteen inches, which is normal for explosives storage areas. However, those parts of the shafts in the mine area which were sealed are known to contain explosives, some of which are visible through apertures in the sealing walls.' John wonders why the official line has been weakened from 'are known to contain explosives' to a more vague 'there may be'.

For some years, nothing grew in the area of the crater, and this led to the legend that no birds sang there. It may have been true for a few years, but today nature has wielded its magic. Perhaps because it is now fenced off, the crater has become a wildlife haven. Trees have been planted, and flora and fauna abound. Over 150 different species of plants have been found, including wild orchids, harebells, bird's foot trefoils, cowslips and perhaps, most appropriately of all, forget-me-nots. There are frogs and newts, dragonflies and damselflies, butterflies and moths. Because of the abundant wildlife, birds have returned, and kingfishers, kestrels, marsh tits, white throats, willow warblers, wood pigeons and chiffchaff have all been seen. Mother Nature is truly a great healer of the physical scars created by man-made catastrophes.

'THEY HAVE HANGED MY SAINTLY BILLY'

———————— ❀ ————————

Many mothers look at their sons through rose-tinted spectacles and see them as lovely boys while the rest of the world regards them as villains. The mother of Dr William Palmer always referred to her son as 'my saintly Billy' even after he was hanged for murder at the age of 31. William, born in Rugeley in 1824, was the second of five brothers. In adulthood they were a mixed lot: Joseph was a wealthy merchant, George a solicitor, Thomas an Anglican clergyman, but Walter ended up a bankrupt alcoholic. William himself eventually became a doctor, but only after a very unsavoury start to his career.

After attending Rugeley Grammar School, where he had the reputation of being a spendthrift on money he had borrowed, he was apprenticed to Evans and Sons, a firm of wholesale chemists in Liverpool. While he was there he seduced the daughter of the family where he lodged. This young lady was the first in a long line of William's conquests, as seduction was a favourite leisure activity that was to become a lifelong interest. However, it was embezzlement rather than sexual adventuring that led to his dismissal. He was caught opening the firm's letters and stealing money. William had spent everything on ladies of the night and betting on horses, but his widowed mother made good the missing money, thus preventing him being taken to court and charged. Evans and Sons were obviously satisfied with this arrangement as they allowed William's brother Thomas to take over the apprenticeship in his place.

William returned to Staffordshire and began a career in medicine by being apprenticed to Dr Edward Tylecote in Great Haywood. He was still very fond of seduction, and was ingenious in some of the methods he employed to be alone with the girls he fancied. He made a point of attending church regularly, but frequently arranged to be called out of the service to attend a sick patient. In reality, he was visiting his young mistress, Jane Widnall, while her parents remained safely ensconced for an hour or more in the church he had just left. At Great Haywood, he again practised his dishonest habits, cheating patients out of their money, and once again, his mother had to restore the money he had stolen.

He next took up work at Stafford Infirmary, and was suspected of poisoning a man named Abley who had challenged Palmer to a drinking competition. Although nothing was proved, the infirmary brought in a new order forbidding students from entering the dispensary where the poisons were kept.

In 1846 William was sent to complete his training under a Dr Stegall in London. While in the metropolis, William lived a wild life of partying, gambling and womanising. One anxious hospital official refused to give William lodgings in his house, stating that he had the moral welfare of his daughters to consider. Given William's extravagant and licentious lifestyle, it is somewhat surprising that he succeeded in completing his medical training and gained the Diploma of the College of Surgeons. It may be less surprising to learn that he failed to pay Dr Stegall the 50 guineas he had promised him for helping him pass his exams!

Dr Palmer returned to his native Rugeley and set up practice in a house in Market Street. He soon began to pay court to an 18-year-old girl named Ann Brookes who lived with her guardian, Charles Dawson, in Abbots Bromley. Ann had been left a considerable sum of money by her late

Dr William Palmer.

father, a colonel in the Indian Army, and this may well have been why William decided that on this occasion he would marry the girl. Despite Charles Dawson's misgivings, Ann fell for the blandishments of William Palmer, who could charm the birds off the trees if he set his mind to it. William and Ann were married at the village church in Abbots Bromley in October 1847.

William Palmer had always been fond of horse-racing, and now, in spite of the fact that his medical practice was not making him much money, he established a stable of race-horses, and arranged for them to be trained in Hednesford. His racing enterprises lost money continuously, and Dr Palmer's debts grew larger.

A year after her marriage, Ann Palmer gave birth to a son. Four later children all died as babies, and their nurse, Ann Bradshaw, stated publicly that she believed that Dr Palmer had killed them by putting sugar laced with poison on his finger for them to suck, because he couldn't afford to provide for them.

Other people connected with William Palmer also died unexpectedly, including an illegitimate child of his, which died shortly after he had examined it. Palmer's mother-in-law died while visiting Palmer, immediately after lending him money. Mr Bladon of Ashby-de-la-Zouch visited Dr Palmer in May 1850 to collect some debts; he died during the visit and was buried very promptly. While at a race meeting, Dr Palmer gave medical attention to Mr Bly of Norfolk, to whom he owed £800. When Bly died, Palmer denied owing the money and told the dead man's wife that the debt was owed the other way, to himself.

It was at about this time that William Palmer insured his wife's life for £13,000. When she was taken ill in 1854, Dr Palmer asked an 80-year-old colleague, Dr Bamford, to attend her, but he also continued to prescribe for her himself. Ann Palmer died, and her death was recorded as being caused by cholera. Although William appeared to mourn his wife's death, shedding many tears at her funeral, it has to be noted that the 18-year-old housemaid, Eliza Tharme, bore him an illegitimate child just nine months after Ann's death. The baby was born in Dr Palmer's house but died six months later.

The £13,000 insurance money from Ann's death was soon dissipated, and William tried to insure his brother Walter for £80,000. The insurance companies were suspicious of this large amount, and the eventual sum assured was considerably smaller. Even so, when Walter Palmer died very soon after the insurance was taken out, the company refused to pay. When Palmer tried to insure the life of a friend, George Bate, he could find no company willing to accept the proposal.

William was now desperate to obtain money. Apart from his many debts, he was being blackmailed by Jane Bergen, a young lady with whom he had had a torrid affair. Jane was threatening to show his love letters to her father, a Stafford policeman. These love letters, now stored at Stafford County Record Office, are very frank and salacious, referring frequently to their sexual activities.

One of Dr Palmer's racing cronies was John Parsons Cook of Lutterworth. Like Palmer, Cook was a professional man – he had trained as a solicitor – who preferred to spend his time and money at the racecourse. When one of Cook's horses won the Shrewsbury Handicap, it netted him £1,700, a sum which the impecunious Dr Palmer eyed covetously. After a celebration party in Shrewsbury, the two men returned to Rugeley. Cook took a room in a hotel that was situated opposite Palmer's house.

Dr Palmer invited John to dinner, but after the meal the visitor was taken violently ill. The next day, William sent his sick friend some broth but he was unable to eat it. A chambermaid thought it a pity to waste the broth and drank some, but it caused her to be sick. Palmer sent for the elderly Dr Bamford again, who prescribed some pills for John

Cook. Palmer took pains to draw attention to the handwriting on the pill box, commenting on Dr Bamford's beautiful script. During the night Cook became desperately ill again, shrieking and having convulsions until his body contorted into a rigid curve. He died in agony. William Palmer certified that his friend had died from apoplexy, and arranged for the body to be laid out immediately.

When Cook's stepfather, William Stevens, arrived from Lutterworth, he suspected that Dr Palmer had removed money and papers from the dead man. At the postmortem, Cook's intestines and stomach were pronounced 'healthy' but Stevens insisted that the organs be sent to London for further analysis. The driver of the carriage engaged to transport the jar containing the organs was to claim later that Palmer offered him a bribe of £10 to upset the jar and spill its contents. Palmer seemed very anxious to know the result of the second analysis of Cook's stomach, and bribed the Rugeley postmaster Samuel Cheshire to open the letter from London containing the result. When he read that no poison had been found, William Palmer said, 'I knew it. I'm as innocent as a baby.'

When the Rugeley coroner received a gift of poultry from Dr Palmer, this was seen as another bribe. The inquest heard that Dr Palmer had bought strychnine just before Cook's death and, despite the absence of poison in the corpse, a verdict of wilful murder was brought in.

William Palmer was arrested, and an order was made for the exhumation of his late wife and his brother. Their bodies were examined by Dr Alfred Taylor of Guy's Hospital; he concluded that Ann had probably died of antimony poisoning, though the evidence in the case of Walter Palmer was inconclusive.

However, it was for the murder of John Parsons Cook that Dr Palmer was tried. He should have been tried in Stafford, but because of the strong local feelings against Palmer, the Lord Chancellor brought in a bill to enable offenders to be tried away from the scene of their alleged crime, in certain circumstances. This bill was passed and became known as the Palmer Act. It is still in force.

The trial of Dr William Palmer was therefore held at the Old Bailey in London, where the prosecution was led by the Attorney-General. The top medical men of the country were called on to give evidence on one side or the other. All of the evidence against Palmer was circumstantial, the prosecution case resting on the similarity between the symptoms shown by Cook as he died and those known to be caused by strychnine poisoning. Although the medical witnesses gave differing opinions on the cause of John Cook's death, Sir Benjamin Brodie, the president of the Royal College of Surgeons, stated that Cook's symptoms were unlike any form of natural disease and indicated that he had been given strychnine. This evidence, together with the fact that Dr Palmer had purchased strychnine before Cook's death, weighed heavily on the jury. After a twelve-day trial, William Palmer was found guilty of murder and sentenced by the judge, Lord Chief Justice Campbell, to be taken back to Stafford to be hanged in public.

Palmer maintained his innocence to the last, refusing attempts by the prison chaplain to persuade him to confess for the good of his soul. His brother, the Rev Thomas Palmer, petitioned for a reprieve on the grounds that it was wrong to hang a man on purely circumstantial evidence, but these moves failed.

At 8 am, on Saturday 14th June 1856, William Palmer was taken out to the scaffold, which had been erected outside Stafford prison. Crowds had been gathering since 3 am; some were local people though many had travelled to Stafford by train, by carriage, on horseback or on foot. Some were still suffering from the effects of the previous night's heavy drinking in the local hostelries. Pickpockets were busy, using the occasion of such a sizable crowd for a good day's work, despite the fact that theft could lead to the gallows. Nonconformist preachers were handing out religious tracts, and there were several placards carried aloft with biblical texts written on them. Others were just there for the entertainment, the spectacle, the thrill of being at such an important public event. In all, the crowd numbered over 30,000 people. The more well-to-do had managed to get themselves a good viewpoint on balconies and raised platforms; some carried telescopes.

Palmer took his place in the grim procession, which included the Chief Constable, the High Sheriff, the prison governor and the chaplain. The condemned man was bareheaded, and wore a coarse jacket provided by the prison. He appeared the calmest person present. He climbed the steps of the scaffold to meet a man dressed in a white smock and top hat. This was George Smith, the hangman. Smith was himself a former inmate of Stafford prison who had volunteered to act as assistant hangman at the execution of James Owen and George Thomas sixteen years earlier (see 'Death on the Canal'), and had since worked his way up to official hangman.

William Palmer shook hands with Smith, who then proceeded to place the rope around the doctor's neck, and a white hood over his face. The bolt was drawn and Palmer dropped to his death. His mother, who knew her son's vices only too well, never accepted his guilt on the murder charge. It was at this point that she came out with the wonderful comment, 'They have hanged my saintly Billy.' Some scholars agree with her that Palmer's conviction may have been unsafe. Robert Graves is one who believes that the doctor's appalling record as an serial embezzler, womaniser and reckless gambler made the public only too willing to believe him capable of killing, even though there was no real evidence that Cook had in fact been murdered.

There is one wry footnote to the case. After the Palmer case, a number of eminent Rugeley men became disturbed that the name of their town would always be associated with 'Palmer the Poisoner'. They petitioned the prime minister of the day to ask whether Rugeley could be known by a different name. The prime minister – a man not previously known for his sense of humour – replied that he was prepared to allow their request but only if the town could be named after him. The good burghers considered this alternative – Palmerston – and decided that they could live with the good old name of Rugeley after all!

THE ENIGMA CODE BOOK SNATCH

———— ❁ ————

Colin Grazier was a young Royal Navy sailor from the Two Gates area of Tamworth. Two days after his wedding to his childhood sweetheart in 1942, he returned to his ship, HMS *Petard*, but he never came back. He was killed on active service on 30th October. In her book *Hijacking Enigma*, Christine Large, the director of Bletchley Park Trust, states that the actions of Colin Glazier and his two companions on the day of his death strongly influenced the outcome of the Second World War. When Christine came to Tamworth to talk to the local Royal Naval Association in April 2004, she reiterated this claim. Those of us who were fortunate enough to be in the audience heard her estimate that the actions of Colin Grazier, Antony 'Jimmy' Fasson and Tommy Brown on the night of 30th October 1942 had shortened the war by two years.

Bletchley Park was, of course, the secret location where the leading analytical thinkers of the country – mathematicians, linguists, crossword solvers, bridge players and chessmasters – spent the war decoding the signals and messages used by the enemy. Bletchley Park, also known as Station X, remained top secret throughout the war. Winston Churchill was referring to this, as well as to the wonderful work done there, when he said that the staff at the Bletchley Park were 'the golden geese that laid the golden eggs but never cackled'. It is remarkable that Station X was never

Colin Grazier (from the monument).

once bombed throughout the war; the Luftwaffe remained ignorant of its location.

One of the main tasks at Bletchley Park was the attempt to crack the codes, or more correctly the ciphers, used by the German Enigma machines. Invented in 1918, Enigma machines were first used in 1926, and different versions of Enigma were employed in the German railway system, as well as the army, navy and airforce.

The machines were electro-mechanical devices, with a keyboard like a typewriter, and were used to encipher and decipher messages. Behind the keyboard was a lampboard made up of 26 small circular apertures, each of which would light up when a letter on the keyboard was pressed, and behind the lampboard was the scrambler unit. This consisted of a fixed wheel at each end with a space for three rotating wheels. When a letter key was pressed, any other letter could light up, and it would be over 16,000 keystrokes before the same sequence would be repeated. The German authorities were convinced that the cipher system used in the Enigma machines was completely secure. When a fourth rotary wheel was added to the machine, its complexity was vastly increased. The chance of anyone cracking its cipher by chance were 150 million million million to one!

The staff of Bletchley Park were the people who undertook the vital task of cracking the Enigma cipher. They had a small number of the three-rotor machines and had devised a machine known as a Bombe to help with the task. The Bombe could perform several hundreds of computations a minute and was in fact an early form of computer. Bletchley Park had 26 of them, but each department or hut at Bletchley competed to commandeer as many of them as possible. In 1940 the codebreakers of Hut 6 had succeeded in cracking the cipher used by the Luftwaffe, but that used by the German navy was proving more difficult. The Germans called this cipher 'Triton', but the Bletchley staff had christened it 'Shark'. It was vital that Shark be broken, in order to read the German instructions to its submarines, which were wreaking havoc in the Atlantic, sinking British convoy ships at will.

On 30th October 1942, HMS *Petard* was one of five of British destroyers and an RAF plane that had located a U-boat – the U559 – in the eastern Mediterranean. The plane had spotted a periscope and had dropped depth charges, but these had caused the U-boat to dive for cover. The five ships formed a circle round the spot and used their Asdic, an echo-sounding device, to try to pinpoint the sub. After an hour, they heard a telltale ping, and *Petard* launched depth charges into the sea. Two other destroyers joined in and the game of cat and mouse continued for ten hours. The depth charges had a maximum depth of 500 feet, and the U559 seemed to be hiding below that. The crew of the *Petard* improvised a way of stuffing soap into the holes of the depth charge primers to enable them to sink lower before exploding. Ten of these soaped charges were dropped and they did the trick. The U-boat was disturbed and began to move, triggering the Asdic in the ships above. The destroyers now knew exactly where the German sub was.

The U559 had been damaged by the 300 depth charges, its starboard plates holed as well as its bows. Eventually it blew its tanks and came to the surface. The *Petard's* searchlights picked out the stricken sub, and the conning tower was fired on until the submariners were seen to be abandoning ship and jumping into the sea.

Aboard the *Petard*, Lieutenant Fasson and Able Seaman Colin Grazier stripped off and swam to the submarine. They were followed by a 16-year-old civilian canteen assistant named Tommy Brown, who had lied about his age to go to sea. Grazier and Fasson boarded the U-boat and descended the conning tower. Once inside and standing in rising water, the two men worked by torchlight, smashing open glass cabinets and drawers to get at books and documents. They passed these up to Tommy who was standing on the top of the sub, and he in turn passed then to the men on the *Petard's* whaleboat, which was now alongside. Grazier and Fasson went down a second time and again passed books and papers up to Tommy Brown. On their third descent into the submarine, they attempted to rescue an instrument, possibly an Enigma machine, which was fastened to the wall. As they began to send this up to the surface, the U559 began to sink. Tommy shouted a warning to Grazier and Fasson, but it was too late. A rush of water down the conning tower prevented them from escaping, and the U-boat sank, taking the two men with it. They were lost, drowned inside the German submarine.

Brown returned to the *Petard* in the whaling boat with the material the lost men had liberated. After pausing to haul aboard fourteen exhausted German survivors from the sea, HMS *Petard* sailed for the port of Haifa. From there, the material from the U559 was sent back to England and to Hut 8 at Bletchley Park.

The three heroes, two of them now dead, had managed to capture a current signal book and current weather ciphers. These were enough to give the Bletchley codebreakers, led by Alan Turing, what they needed to crack the four-rotor Enigma ciphers. By 13th December they had done it: the Shark was tamed. Bletchley could now decipher all the codes that Germany was sending to its U-boats and ships. The British navy could now track and destroy the enemy submarines, and the convoys bringing food to Britain could cross the Atlantic more safely.

It was very important that the Germans should not know that their codes had been broken. A year after the action, Tamworth's Colin Grazier and Lieutenant Fasson were given posthumous George Crosses, and the civilian Tommy Brown the George Medal. Given their contribution to the outcome of the war, these would probably have been the Victoria Cross, but VCs are so rare that their award would have drawn too much attention to their heroism. The secret might have got out, and the enemy would have changed their codes again.

Tommy Brown survived the action in the Mediterranean, but was tragically killed in 1945 while attempting to rescue his sister from a tenement fire in North Shields.

For over five decades, the heroism of Colin Glazier went unrecognised in his home town of Tamworth. Then, in 1999, a number of local people began a campaign to have the name of Colin Grazier and his heroic actions of 1942 made public. Led by Phil Shanahan, the deputy editor of the *Tamworth Herald*, and by members of the Tamworth branch of the Royal Navy Association, the campaign held fund raising events and sold copies of a commemorative plate. In four years, the fund raised over £17,700 for a permanent monument.

Today the name of Colin Grazier is celebrated in his home town and far beyond. In November 2000, Phil Shanahan,

Tamworth's monument to the three heroes.

now chairman of the Colin Grazier Memorial Committee, attended an event organised by the Celebrities Guild of Great Britain. There he collected an award for the three heroes, the first posthumous award the Guild had ever made, and said that collecting the award on behalf of the three men was the biggest honour of his life.

In Tamworth, there is a Colin Grazier Hotel, a Grazier Avenue, and even a beer named in honour of the hero. In December 2004, EDS Commercial, an international IT services company, decided to name their Tamworth offices 'Grazier House'.

However, the most prestigious memorial is the magnificent sculpture in St Editha's Square, Tamworth, close to the town's main church. This was designed by Walenty Pytel, one of Europe's leading sculptors. It consists of three anchors linked together by a genuine ship's anchor chain. It was unveiled on Sunday 27th October 2003, just a matter of days under 61 years from the event it commemorates.

At the unveiling were relatives of the three heroes and 35 members from HMS *Petard*, including fourteen who were there on the ship on 30th October 1942. Also present were the local MP, the town mayor, the Lord Lieutenant of Staffordshire, and members of the Colin Grazier Memorial Committee. Messages of support from the Duke of York and the Prime Minister were read out.

The three anchors of the monument represent the three naval heroes, Tamworth's Colin Grazier, Lieutenant Tony Fasson and Tommy Brown. From this, it will be noted that Tamworth is not exclusive in its celebration of Colin Grazier; it remembers all three of the heroes. On the housing estate built near to where Colin lived as a boy are streets named after each of the men, as well as the *Petard* and Bletchley Park.

One event that left Tamworth people feeling outraged was the making of a Holywood film called U571, starring Harvey Keitel and Matthew McConaughey. This film retold the story of the rescue of the Enigma code books from a German submarine by three heroic sailors, but in this version they were American sailors in the American navy. To have had the heroes played by American actors might have been acceptable, but to pretend that the heroes *were* Americans was a joke too far, a travesty of history. It is not surprising that the film was never shown in Tamworth! Robert Harris, the British novelist and expert on the Enigma story, described the small nugget of facts in the film as 'a tiny pebble of British truth flung at an onrushing tidal wave of Yankee baloney.'

However, the people of Staffordshire know the truth. Their local sailor and his two companions were the real men who took the heroic action in 1942, and thus shortened the war.

ASSASSINATED IN ERROR

---❖---

Captain Roy Farran, the eldest of four brothers, was a soldier whose wartime exploits in the Special Air Service were both clandestine and heroic. Initially serving with the King's Own Hussars, he joined the SAS at its formation in 1943 and served in Tunisia, Sicily, Greece, Italy and France, frequently operating behind enemy lines. In 1945 he and a handful of men parachuted into Italy to work with the Italian partisans in the Apennine mountains. One audacious feat was

Rex Farran (back row, right). (Mrs N Hill)

when Roy Farran led a successful attack on the German Corps headquarters at Albinea. Roy's wartime heroism was recognised by the award of the French Croix de Guerre, the American Legion of Merit, and in Britain by the Military Cross with two bars and the Distinguished Service Order.

After the war, Roy Farran stood in the 1945 general election as the Conservative candidate for the Black Country constituency of Dudley and Stourbridge, though he was not elected. He also wrote an autobiographical account of his wartime exploits in the SAS. This book, entitled *Winged Dagger: Adventures on Special Service*, was scheduled to be published by Collins in 1948.

Later, he became an undercover agent in Palestine, organising the special duties Q Squads, which were formed to investigate and sabotage the activities of the Stern Gang. This organisation was founded in 1940 by Avraham Stern following a split in the underground Irgun movement. The Stern Gang, or 'Lehi', were either violent terrorists or determined 'fighters for the freedom of Israel', depending on who is writing the history. They were fanatically anti-British during World War II and, in contrast to the firmly anti-Nazi Irgun movement, they even invited help from the Axis powers to drive the British out of Palestine!

Although Stern himself was killed by the police in February 1942, his organisation continued its terrorist activities after his death. In November 1944 the Stern Gang assassinated Lord Moyne, a British minister of state. The Irgun too was still active in violent anti-British activity, and in 1946 its members blew up the headquarters of the British administration in Palestine, the King David Hotel in Jerusalem. This atrocity killed 88 people, including Britons, Arabs and Jews.

When the authorities began to flog and to hang captured terrorists, Irgun and the Stern Gang developed a strategy of kidnapping British hostages and retaliating in kind. Although most Jews sympathised with the aim of the establishment of an independent state of Israel after the end of the war, the vast majority disapproved of the terrorists' use of bombs and bullets to achieve this aim.

Roy Farran's Q Squads were formed to fight the terrorist groups at their own game and with their own tactics. When a 15-year-old member of the Stern Gang, Alexander Rubowitz, disappeared after being abducted by a Q Squad on 6th May 1947, this led to a public outcry. In October Captain Roy Farran was tried by a general court martial in Jerusalem, on the charge of murdering the missing boy.

Evidence was given that on 6th May, Alexander Rubowitz had been distributing Stern Gang literature when he was intercepted by members of a Q Squad. Witnesses said that he had been chased by a man, who caught him, bundled him into a saloon car containing two other men, and drove off. The boy had not been seen since, and his parents had been notified that he was 'presumably dead'. During the chase, the man who had caught the youth had lost his hat, which was found later at the scene. This hat was produced in court, and had the letters FAR-AN (with the fourth letter missing) written inside it. A witness also identified Capt Farran as the man who had abducted the missing youth.

Much legal debate took place when Roy Farran's defence counsel objected to the admissibility as evidence of documents written by Capt Farran while in custody, arguing that these were notes written by the accused officer for his defence. They were therefore privileged and could not be used against him. When the court martial ruled in favour of this argument, the defence then argued that as Rubowitz's body had not been found, there was no case to answer. The court martial concurred and acquitted Roy Farran.

However the Stern Gang never accepted the verdict and swore revenge. Graffiti appeared on walls in Tel Aviv and other towns, and leaflets were distributed stating that Captain Farran's time would come, and promising that he would be pursued to the ends of the earth. Capt Farran left

Palestine and returned to live at the family home in Codsall, Staffordshire.

At 8 o'clock on the morning of Monday 3rd May 1948, postwoman Eileen Hayes delivered a parcel to 'The Myron', a house on Histons Hill, Codsall. It was addressed to Captain Roy Farran, but he was away in Scotland, accompanied by a police bodyguard. Eileen Hayes actually handed the parcel over to Roy's 26-year-old brother Rex.

As Eileen went back down the drive, Rex Farran took the parcel into the house. A special brick safety chamber had been installed in the house in which suspicious objects could be placed, but Rex had no occasion to suspect anything was amiss. He could tell that the package contained a book, and immediately thought it must be a copy of *Winged Dagger*. Rex was keen to see a copy of his brother's work, and decided not to wait until his return.

As he opened the parcel, it exploded. The whole house shook, windows were shattered, and Rex Farran received horrendous injuries to his legs and abdomen. He was rushed four miles to the Wolverhampton Royal Hospital for emergency treatment, but died two hours later. His death was later recorded as due to haemorrhage and shock.

Subsequent forensic investigation of the pieces of the parcel proved that it had indeed contained a book. It was not *Winged Dagger* as Rex had assumed, but a copy of the complete plays of William Shakespeare. The book had been hollowed out, and inside it there had been a fragment bomb attached to a battery. The whole thing was a boobytrap device, designed to explode when the parcel was opened.

Police inquiries revealed that the particular edition of Shakespeare plays had been available at many metropolitan and provincial bookshops, and they were unable to find where it had been purchased. The postmark on what remained of the parcel's wrappings showed that it had been posted in the east end of London. Roy Farran informed the police that he had received threatening letters, also posted in

Captain Roy Farran kneels at his brother's grave. His two brothers are behind. (Wolverhampton Express & Star)

east London, the previous October. They had contained a single piece of paper bearing one word – Revenge – written in Hebrew. Scotland Yard detectives began an immediate investigation of all known Stern Gang sympathisers living in London. They also checked recent immigration records against a list of Stern Gang members, and asked other European police forces to do the same.

Although the police could find no direct evidence linking the Stern Gang with the killing, a British news agency in Paris received a telephone call the day after the murder. The caller claimed to be a Stern Gang spokesman and said that the killing had been their response to the British government's decision to send further troops to Palestine, as well as a personal revenge for the death of Alexander Rubowitz.

If the call was genuine – and it was widely accepted that it was – then the personal revenge aimed at Roy Farran killed the wrong man, a young engineering draughtsman who had absolutely no connection with the politics of the Middle East. Joan Cooper was a friend of the Farran family, and she remembers Rex as being cheerful and likeable. Joan's husband and Rex Farran were both employed at the Boulton & Paul aircraft factory in Wolverhampton, and they were all together at the firm's social club the night before the killing. It was a warm evening, and they were sitting outside having a drink. Joan recalls Rex Farran sitting her one-year-old son on his knee and playing with him. 'He was a wonderful young man,' she told me, 'always smiling. We just could not believe it when he was killed by the letter bomb the next day. What sort of people could do that to someone like Rex?' Vince Cresswell, who played in the same works' football team as the murdered man, recalls that whether the team won or lost, Rex never complained or bragged about the result.

Rex Farran's funeral was held in Codsall on Friday 7th May, and was attended by his parents and brothers, his former colleagues from Boulton & Paul, his soccer team-mates, and his many friends. Together they all mourned the loss of a young man who, in the words of Vince Cresswell, 'never made an enemy in his life'.

Captain Roy Farran, whose younger brother had been blown up by a bomb aimed at him, later emigrated to Canada, where he became a newspaper proprietor in Calgary.

MYSTERIES OF THE SHEPHERDS' MONUMENT

❁

Shugborough Hall is situated in the centre of Staffordshire, and is the home of the 5th Earl of Lichfield, better known as the photographer Patrick Lichfield. It is part of a historic estate, with a working farm, dairy, water mill, brewhouse and kitchens, and it is visited by a quarter of a million people every year.

In Shugborough Park there is a most mysterious monument, which was erected in the mid-18th century and was designed by Thomas Wright who was a mathematician, an instrument

Shugborough Hall. (Lesley Hextall)

Detail of the carving on the Shepherd's Monument. (Lesley Hextall)

maker and an astronomer. Doric columns and a crest were added later. It is known as the Shepherds' Monument because of the marble relief of shepherds and shepherdesses, carved by

Dutch sculptor Peter Scheemakers, which is based on a *Les Bergers d'Arcadie*, a painting by Nicolas Poussin. The monument was commissioned in 1748 by Admiral Thomas Anson, one of Patrick Lichfield's ancestors.

Poussin was rumoured to be a Grand Master of the Knights Templar so it is not surprising that *Les Bergers d'Arcadie* has always been the subject of speculation. Its layout has been connected with the secrets of the Knights Templar, traditionally the keepers of the secrets of the Holy Grail. The legends of the Holy Grail, or Sangreal, have fascinated scholars for centuries, and have connections with both Christian and Celtic myths. It has been said to be a chalice, a dish, a Celtic bowl of plenty, or even a pagan fertility cauldron.

In the best-known account of the Holy Grail, it is the vessel from which Jesus drank at the Last Supper. It came into the possession of Joseph of Arimathea, said to be Jesus's uncle, who caught some of Christ's blood in it at the crucifixion. Joseph later brought the vessel to England where it provided him with food, drink and spiritual sustenance for the rest of his life. In one version of the legend, it passed down through Joseph's descendants and was later owned by Sir Galahad, one of King Arthur's knights. At some time it disappeared, and thousands of searchers, including the Knights of the Round Table and the Knights Templar, have been trying to discover its whereabouts ever since. It is said that only someone of absolute purity – like Sir Galahad himself – will be able to find the Grail. The search for the Holy Grail has become such a timeless legend that the phrase is today used for any seeking after ultimate truth or knowledge.

One variation of the story states that the legend of a holy chalice derives from a mistranslation. It was not the *san greal*, but the *sang real*, the bloodline of Jesus Christ. In his book *Bloodline of the Holy Grail*, Laurence Gardner postulates that Jesus Christ did not die on the cross, but survived to marry Mary Magdalene and to have children. It was the son of Christ who was brought to England by Joseph of Arimathea (who in this version of the legend was the younger brother of Jesus, not his uncle as tradition has it). The quest for the Holy Grail is therefore the search for the lineage of Jesus's bloodline, not a search for a physical artefact. Gardner traces the lineage through various Welsh, Breton and Scottish kings and through the Stuart kings of England. (Not surprisingly, the foreword to his book is written by Prince Michael of Albany, the current Stuart claimant to the throne.) The researches of Laurence Gardner and many others have been used in the best-selling novel, *The Da Vinci Code*.

However, it is probably the drinking vessel that most people have in mind when examining the monument at Shugborough. Scholars had often seen clues to the location of the Grail in the geometry of Poussin's painting, and in the arcane Masonic symbols within it, and it is not surprising that these beliefs have been transferred to the version of it on the Shepherds' Monument in Shugborough Park. There are differences between the painting and the sculpture. The most obvious is that the likeness on the Staffordshire monument is a mirror image of the original painting; the whole picture is reversed. There are minor changes too. In the painting one shepherd is pointing his forefinger, but on the relief picture the hands of both shepherds are clenched, so that only the thumbs are raised, the fingers being hidden inside the fist. Is this another Masonic symbol? Also, Poussin has one shepherd pointing to the word ARCADIA, thought by some to mean Nova Scotia. At Shugborough the shepherd's thumb is between the letters R and C, thus splitting up the word. Yet another mystery.

The Staffordshire monument has a further enigma in the letters under the Poussin reverse image. On one line are: O U O S V A V V, and beneath these are the letter D on the extreme left and M on the right. These letters have puzzled visitors from Charles Darwin to Josiah Wedgwood, and they continue to mystify researchers today. In May 2004 Shugborough invited codebreakers from Bletchley Park, where the codes connected with the wartime Enigma machines were cracked, to investigate the inscription. Many other people have tried too.

Margaret, Countess of Lichfield and the grandmother of Patrick Lichfield, always believed that the mysterious letters referred to a love poem she learned as a young girl. In a letter written in 1987, she spoke about a young curate who used to tell her stories of Greek and Roman myths. She recalled a poem he told her about a Roman shepherdess named Alicia, which contained the words: 'Out of your own sweet vale, Alicia, vanish vanity twixt Deity and Man, thou shepherdess the way.' The Countess may have been convinced of this explanation, but no one has been able to track down the poem or any tale about Alicia. They wonder whether the curate had in fact made up the poem to match the mystery letters. People have sought other solutions, via both Freemasonry and the Jewish Kabbalah.

Flippant souls have put forward amusing answers including one from a football fan who suggested that it was a Georgian fixture list that read: Deepdale, Old Trafford, Upton Park, Oakwell, St Andrews, Villa Park, Anfield, Vale

The enigmatic letters on the Shepherd's Monument. (Lesley Hextall)

Park, Valley Parade and the Madejski Stadium. An equally obsessed soccer fan thought it might be an ancient Scottish football formation with two up front and a flat back eight!

More serious codebreakers have suggested that to understand what the Shepherds' Monument might mean, it is necessary to take into account not only the letters, but also the image of the shepherds, the geometry of the shepherds' hands and staffs, the ET IN ARCADIA EGO inscription on the picture, and its position within other monuments at Shugborough Park.

Bletchley Park veteran codebreakers Oliver and Sheila Lawn, who worked there during the war, found the task difficult. On his first visit to see the monument, Oliver stated, 'I think you need classical knowledge as well as ingenuity. It is totally different from what I used to do during the war. This is a language rather than a mathematical code. We need a bit more intelligence about the Anson family. There is always a key, but if this was a code between two people and only they knew it, it could be almost impossible to decipher.' Nevertheless, the Bletchley Park team persevered, and in November 2004 they announced that they thought that it might be a secret message from an 18th century Christian sect known as the Priory of Sion. The decoded message appears to say 'Jesus (as Deity) Defy' and refers to their belief that Jesus was an earthly prophet rather than a divinity. They had to keep their views secret – and their messages cryptic – because they were regarded as heretical by the Church authorities. The Priory is not a building but a clandestine society, and although the Bletchley Park research refers to it as an 18th century sect, the Priory of Sion traces its pedigree back to 1090, and over the centuries its grand masters have included Leonardo da Vinci, Isaac Newton, Victor Hugo, Claude Debussy and Jean Cocteau.

Oliver Lawn's findings bear out work done by an American defence cryptanalyst, who used methods including letter frequency, decryption matrices, and language study. He found that the key that could unlock the code was the number 1223. This codebreaker visited the monument after his analytical work and found that the number was faintly inscribed on it several times over. Using the setting 1223, he found that after anagramming the words 'Jesus H Defy' emerge.

However, it has to be said that there are as many theories as there are researchers. The Shepherds' Monument at Shugborough has been claimed by ufologists (there have been many UFOs spotted in this part of Staffordshire), students of Nostradamus, believers in the ways of Wicca (Shugborough actually means place of the witch), Jacobite sympathisers, numerologists and alchemists, as well as those seeking clues to the location of the Holy Grail. There are those who claim that the monument points to the Grail being in England, in Turkey, and even in Nova Scotia. Admiral Thomas Anson who commissioned the monument did visit Nova Scotia himself, and there is that reference to Arcadia, the old name for that part of the world. Then there are others who claim that it is simply a secret message between lovers.

The mysteries remain. Richard Kemp, the estate manager at Shugborough, says, 'It's like Everest, you climb it because it's there. There's a code here, so everyone wants to unravel it.'

BIBLIOGRAPHY

———— ❁ ————

Bell, David *Staffordshire and the Black Country Murder Casebook* (Countryside Books 1996)

Bell, David *Ghosts and Legends of Staffordshire and the Black Country* (Countryside Books 1994)

Boda, Shari-Jayne *Real Crime* (Granada 2003)

Clarke, David *A Guide to Britain's Pagan Heritage* (Hale1995)

Foot, Paul *Murder at the Farm: Who Killed Carl Bridgewater?* (Penguin 1986, revised 1993)

Gardner, Laurence *Bloodline of the Holy Grail* (Element Books Ltd 2000)

Graves, Robert *They Hanged My Saintly Billy* (Cassell 1957)

Hackwood, F.W. *Staffordshire: Customs, Superstitions & Folklore* (Mercury Press 1924)

Harpur, Stephen *Capturing Enigma* (Sutton Publication 1999)

Harrison, Paul *Shropshire Murder Casebook* (Countryside Books 1994)

Kent, Jeff *The Mysterious Double Sunset* (Witan Books 2001)

Large, Christine *Highjacking Enigma: the Insider's Tale* (John Wiley & Sons 2003)

Pickford, Doug *Myths & Legends of East Cheshire & the Moorlands* (Sigma Leisure 1992)

Pickford, Doug *Magic, Myth & Memories in and around the Peak District* (Sigma Press 1993)

Pickford, Doug *Staffordshire: Its Magic & Mystery* (Sigma Press 1994)

Pickford, Doug *Earth Mysteries of the Three Shires* (Churnet Valley Books 1996)

Pipe, Marian *Secret Staffordshire* (SB Publications 1994)

Rice, Marcia Alice *Abbots Bromley* (Wilding & Son 1939)

Rowe, Mark *The Day the Dump Went Up* (Mark Rowe 1999)

Shipman, E.R. *The Abbots Bromley Horn Dance* (Benhill Press Ltd 1982)

ACKNOWLEDGEMENTS

———————— ✾ ————————

Many people helped me while I was writing this book. I would particularly like to thank John Kay, Lesley Hextall, Jeff Kent, Glenys Cooper, Doug Pickford, John Cooper, George Jones, Terry Bailey, Jackie Barfoot, Sheena McDonagh, Irene Turner, Derek Wheelhouse, Reg Bowers, Arnold Gibson, Phil Shanahan, John Harper, John Godwin and John Bould. I would also like to acknowledge assistance given by Biddulph Library, Biddulph & District Genealogy and Historical Society, Burton Library, the *Tamworth Herald*, the *Wolverhampton Express and Star* and Ottakars in Burton.